BETTY CROCKER'S BISQUICK COOKBOOK

Seven mini cookbooks in one with step-by-step recipes

Myrna McCauley, Editor
Harry Heim, Art Director

For the woman
who's practical enough
to take a shortcut
and creative enough to
make the most of it

TABLE OF CONTENTS

It lets you start where the fun begins — *after* the basic ingredients

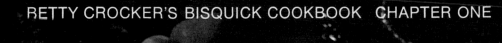

HOLIDAY HOSPITALITY

HOLIDAY HOSPITALITY

Deck the halls! With holly or hearts, shamrocks or bunnies, pumpkins or turkey gobblers. Here comes a bevy of holiday bakings to help you celebrate the happiest days of the year.

These are foods that are first to be admired and then devoured: Spectacular beauties like White Christmas Pie and February's Baked Alaska. Incredible edibles like valentine hearts that turn out to be pizzas and jack-o'-lanterns that are teacakes in disguise. Traditional favorites like holly season nut breads and Easter's Hot Cross Buns. Each of these holiday bakings is easy and fun to do — after all, each one starts with Bisquick® baking mix. And to simplify even further, all of our new recipes are streamlined with step-by-step directions.

So check the calendar, pick your holiday and bake up a little happiness for your family and friends. Then serve with a dash of showmanship — using your prettiest dishes and linens, flowers for the centerpiece maybe, candlelight when appropriate.

Betty Crocker

White Christmas Pie is pictured on the other side of this page. Recipe on page 6.

MINCEMEAT MERRYMAKERS

Easy drop cookies, moist and spicy. Nice with eggnog for holiday parties.

1½ cups prepared mincemeat
¾ cup evaporated milk
3 cups Bisquick baking mix
½ cup brown sugar (packed)
½ tsp salt

Heat oven to 375°

1 Heat mincemeat and milk in large saucepan to simmering, stirring frequently. Cook until slightly thickened, about 10 minutes.

2 Stir in remaining ingredients. (Dough will be soft and sticky.)

3 Drop dough by teaspoonfuls about 2 inches apart onto greased baking sheet.

4 Bake *about 10 minutes* or until light brown. *About 3½ dozen.*

OLD-FASHIONED DATE BARS

For a solid gold setting, spray paint a tray. Cover with a lace paper doily, add a sprig of holly.

¼ cup butter or margarine, softened
¾ cup sugar
1 egg
1⅔ cups Bisquick baking mix
1 cup cut-up dates
½ cup chopped nuts

Heat oven to 350°

1 Mix butter, sugar and egg; stir in remaining ingredients.

2 Spread dough in greased and floured square pan, 9x9x2 inches.

3 Bake *25 to 30 minutes* or until light brown. Cool and cut into bars, 2x1½ inches. If you like, sprinkle with confectioners' sugar. *2 dozen.*

CHERRY FRUIT CHEWS

Moist, rich bars. Good travelers for gifts that go via the postman.

¼ cup butter or margarine, softened
1 cup sugar
2 eggs
1¼ cups Bisquick baking mix
1 cup chopped walnuts
1 cup cut-up dates
1 jar (4 oz) maraschino cherries, drained and chopped (about ⅓ cup)

Heat oven to 350°

1 Mix butter, sugar and eggs; stir in baking mix. Gently fold in nuts, dates and cherries.

2 Spread dough in greased oblong pan, 13x9x2 inches.

3 Bake *30 minutes.* Cool slightly and cut into 1½-inch squares. *4 dozen.*

HOLIDAY NUT BREAD

This one's made with apricots, but you can substitute cut-up dried peaches, dates, raisins or figs instead.

3 cups Bisquick baking mix
⅔ cup sugar
⅓ cup Gold Medal® flour
1 egg
1 cup orange juice
1 cup cut-up dried apricots
¾ cup chopped nuts

Heat oven to 350°

1 Combine baking mix, sugar, flour, egg and orange juice; beat vigorously ½ minute. Stir in apricots and nuts.

2 Pour batter into greased loaf pan, 9x5x3 inches.

3 Bake *55 to 60 minutes* or until wooden pick inserted in center comes out clean. Cool thoroughly before slicing.

GOLDEN PUMPKIN LOAF

Subtly flavored with pumpkin and spices. Festive for a holiday brunch or buffet table.

1 cup sugar
1 egg
1 can (16 oz) pumpkin
3 cups Bisquick baking mix
1 tsp pumpkin pie spice
½ tsp cloves
½ tsp nutmeg

Heat oven to 350°

1 Blend sugar, egg and pumpkin in large mixer bowl on medium speed. Gradually beat in baking mix and spices on low speed.

2 Pour batter into greased loaf pan, 9x5x3 inches.

3 Bake *70 minutes* or until wooden pick inserted in center comes out clean.

CANDIED FRUIT COFFEE BREAD

1 pkg active dry yeast
½ cup warm water (105 to 115°)
1 egg
1 tbsp sugar
2½ cups Bisquick baking mix
½ cup chopped mixed candied fruit
¼ cup chopped nuts
Confectioners' Sugar Icing (below)

1 Dissolve yeast in warm water. Mix in egg, sugar and baking mix; beat vigorously. Stir in fruit and nuts.

2 Drop dough by tablespoonfuls into greased square pan, 8x8x2 inches.

3 Cover and let rise in warm place until double, about 1 hour.

4 Heat oven to 400°. Bake *15 minutes* or until golden brown. Frost with Confectioners' Sugar Icing. *9 servings.*

CONFECTIONERS' SUGAR ICING Blend 1 cup confectioners' sugar, ¼ teaspoon vanilla and 2 to 3 teaspoons water.

CHRISTMAS BISCUIT TREE

Dinner biscuits, flecked with pimiento or parsley, and baked in the shape of a Christmas tree.

2 cups Bisquick baking mix
½ cup cold water
¼ cup chopped pimiento, well drained, or 2 tbsp snipped parsley

Heat oven to 450°

1 Stir all ingredients to a soft dough. Gently smooth dough into a ball on floured cloth-covered board. Knead 5 times.

2 Roll dough ½ inch thick. Cut with floured 2-inch biscuit cutter.

3 Arrange biscuits close together in shape of Christmas tree on aluminum foil-covered baking sheet.

4 Bake *10 to 12 minutes* or until golden brown. Serve warm. *10 biscuits.*

TRIM-A-TREE COFFEE CAKE

2 cups Bisquick baking mix
3 tbsp sugar
⅔ cup orange juice
1 egg
2 tbsp salad oil
Glaze (below)
1 can (11 oz) mandarin orange segments, drained
Maraschino cherry halves

Heat oven to 400°

1 Mix all ingredients except Glaze and fruit; beat vigorously ½ minute.

2 Spread batter in greased round layer pan, 9x1½ inches.

3 Bake *25 to 30 minutes.* Cool 10 minutes.

4 Spread with Glaze. Arrange orange segments and cherry halves on coffee cake to resemble a Christmas tree.

GLAZE Blend ½ cup confectioners' sugar, ¼ teaspoon vanilla and 1 tablespoon water.

WHITE CHRISTMAS PIE

*Pictured on chapter cover.
A dream of a vanilla cream-
coconut pie, served with
raspberry sauce.*

9-INCH SHORT PIE SHELL

1 cup Bisquick baking mix
¼ cup butter or margarine,
    softened
3 tbsp boiling water

Heat oven to 450°

1 Combine baking mix and
butter in small bowl. Add
water; stir vigorously until
dough forms a ball and cleans
the bowl. (Dough will be puffy
and soft.)

2 Pat dough with floured hands
into 9-inch pie pan, bringing
up dough to edge of pan.
If you like, flute edge.

3 Bake *8 to 10 minutes.* Cool.

FILLING & SAUCE

1 envelope (about 2 oz) dessert
    topping mix
1 can (3½ oz) flaked coconut
1 can (18 oz) Betty Crocker®
    vanilla pudding
1 tbsp orange-flavored liqueur
    or orange juice
½ cup raspberry jam

Prepare topping mix as
directed on package. Gently
fold topping and 1 cup of the
coconut into pudding. Pour
pudding mixture into pie shell.
Sprinkle with remaining
coconut. Chill at least 2 hours
or until set. Stir liqueur into
jam and serve in small bowl
as topping.

PIE ON A PEDESTAL For
holiday flair, bring your pie to
the table on a cake pedestal.
Cut and serve before your
guests.

VELVET PUMPKIN CAKE

*A one-layer beauty, served
warm in a snowdrift of
whipped cream.*

1½ cups Bisquick baking mix
½ cup sugar
¾ cup pumpkin pie mix
1 egg
2 tbsp shortening
1 tsp vanilla
Sweetened whipped cream

Heat oven to 350°

1 Blend all ingredients except
whipped cream in large mixer
bowl on low speed ½ minute,
scraping bowl frequently. Beat
4 minutes medium speed.

2 Pour batter into greased and
floured square pan, 8x8x2
inches, or round layer pan,
9x1½ inches.

3 Bake *35 to 40 minutes* or until
wooden pick inserted in center
comes out clean. Serve warm
with whipped cream. *9 servings.*

TURKEY POT PIE

*Lucky enough to have
leftovers? Try this rich, meaty
one-crust pie and toss a salad.*

Turkey Filling (right)
2 cups Bisquick baking mix
2 tbsp shortening
⅓ cup milk

Heat oven to 450°

1 Prepare Turkey Filling. Pour
into ungreased baking dish,
11½x7½x1½ inches. Keep
hot in oven while preparing
topping.

2 Stir remaining ingredients to
a soft dough. Gently smooth
dough into a ball on floured
cloth-covered board. Knead
5 times.

3 Pat or roll dough into a
rectangle, 11x7 inches. Cut
2 or 3 slits in center and place
over hot filling.

4 Bake *about 15 minutes. 4 to
6 servings.*

TURKEY FILLING

¼ cup chopped onion
¼ cup butter or margarine
⅓ cup Bisquick baking mix
1 tsp salt
½ tsp pepper
2 cups chicken broth*
⅔ cup light cream
3 to 4 cups cut-up cooked turkey
1 tbsp chopped pimiento
1 tsp Worcestershire sauce

Cook and stir onion in butter
in large saucepan until tender.
Blend in baking mix, salt and
pepper. Cook over low heat,
stirring until mixture is bubbly.
Remove from heat. Stir in
remaining ingredients. Heat to
boiling, stirring constantly.
Boil and stir 1 minute.

*Chicken broth can be made
by dissolving 2 chicken
bouillon cubes in 2 cups
boiling water, or use canned
chicken broth.

TURKEY CASSEROLE

2 cans (10½ oz each) condensed
  cream of celery soup
¾ cup milk
1½ cups cooked vegetables
3 cups cut-up cooked turkey
2 cups Bisquick baking mix
½ cup cold water
½ cup cranberry sauce

Heat oven to 450°

1 Heat soup and milk, stirring
frequently. Stir in vegetables
and turkey; heat through.

2 Pour mixture into ungreased
3-quart casserole. Keep hot in
oven while preparing topping.

3 Stir baking mix and water to a
soft dough. Gently smooth
dough into a ball on floured
cloth-covered board. Knead
5 times.

4 Roll dough into a rectangle,
12x9 inches; spread with
cranberry sauce. Roll up,
beginning at wide side; cut into
1-inch slices. Place slices cut
side down on hot turkey mixture.

5 Bake uncovered *20 minutes*
or until biscuits are golden
brown. *6 to 8 servings.*

FEBRUARY'S BAKED ALASKA

Strawberry spectacular on a shortcake to dazzle a dozen valentines.

2⅓ cups Bisquick baking mix
3 tbsp sugar
⅔ cup light cream
1 qt strawberry ice cream
Meringue (right)

Heat oven to 450°

1 Stir baking mix, sugar and cream to a soft dough. Pat dough into greased round layer pan, 8x1½ inches.

2 Bake *12 to 15 minutes.* Remove from pan and cool thoroughly.

3 Line bowl 1 inch smaller than cake diameter with aluminum foil. Pack ice cream into bowl; freeze until firm.

4 Cover baking sheet with aluminum foil; place shortcake on baking sheet. Invert bowl with ice cream onto shortcake; remove bowl and foil. Freeze shortcake and ice cream.

5 Just before serving, *heat oven to 500°.* Completely cover shortcake and ice cream with Meringue, sealing it to foil on sheet.

6 Bake *3 to 5 minutes* or until light brown. Trim foil to edge of Meringue; transfer to serving plate. Serve immediately. *12 servings.*

MERINGUE   Beat 4 egg whites and ½ teaspoon cream of tartar until foamy. Beat in ½ cup sugar, 1 tablespoon at a time; continue beating until stiff and glossy. Do not underbeat. Beat in ½ teaspoon vanilla.

SWEETHEART PIZZA TRIO

2½ cups Bisquick baking mix
1 pkg active dry yeast
⅔ cup hot water
2 cans (8 oz each) tomato sauce
½ cup chopped onion
1 cup grated Parmesan cheese
2 tsp oregano
¼ tsp pepper
2 cups shredded Cheddar or
   mozzarella cheese (about 8 oz)
2 cups sliced pepperoni

Heat oven to 425°

1 Stir together baking mix and yeast; add water and beat vigorously.

2 Turn dough onto well-floured board and knead until smooth, about 20 times. Allow dough to rest a few minutes.

3 Divide dough into three parts. Roll each part about ¼ inch thick on ungreased baking sheet. Shape each into heart; pinch edge to make slight rim.

4 Spread tomato sauce almost to edge of each heart. Layer with remaining ingredients.

5 Bake *15 to 20 minutes. 3 pizzas.*

HEARTY CHICKEN CASSEROLE

Creamed chicken with heart-shape biscuits for a Valentine supper by candlelight.

Creamed Chicken (right)
1 cup Bisquick baking mix
2 tbsp chopped pimiento,
   drained
2 to 3 tbsp water

Heat oven to 450°

1 Prepare Creamed Chicken. Pour into ungreased 2-quart casserole. Keep hot in oven while preparing biscuits.

2 Stir remaining ingredients to a soft dough. Gently smooth dough into a ball on floured cloth-covered board. Knead 5 times.

3 Roll dough ¼ inch thick. Cut with floured 2-inch heart-shape cutter. Place biscuits on hot chicken mixture.

4 Bake *about 15 minutes* or until biscuits are golden brown. *4 to 6 servings.*

CREAMED CHICKEN

¼ cup butter or margarine
¼ cup Bisquick baking mix
½ tsp salt
¼ tsp pepper
2 cups milk
2 cups cut-up cooked chicken

Melt butter over low heat in saucepan. Blend in baking mix and seasonings. Cook over low heat, stirring until mixture is smooth and bubbly. Remove from heat and stir in milk. Heat to boiling, stirring constantly. Boil and stir 1 minute. Stir in chicken and heat through.

NOTE Use Bisquick baking mix for all your sauces and gravies. For breading chicken, too.

WASHINGTON'S CHERRY NUT BREAD

By George, it's a cheery cherry beauty — bulging with candied cherries and spiced with cardamom.

3 cups Bisquick baking mix
½ cup sugar
⅓ cup Gold Medal flour*
1 tsp ground cardamom
1 egg
1 cup milk
1 cup candied cherries, cut up
¾ cup chopped nuts

Heat oven to 350°

1 Combine baking mix, sugar, flour, cardamom, egg and milk; beat vigorously ½ minute. Stir in cherries and nuts.

2 Pour batter into greased loaf pan, 9x5x3 inches.

3 Bake *55 to 60 minutes* or until wooden pick inserted in center comes out clean. Cool thoroughly before slicing.

*Do not use self-rising flour in this recipe.

LINCOLN'S LOG

2 eggs
⅔ cup granulated sugar
1 tsp vanilla
¼ cup milk
1 cup Bisquick baking mix
Confectioners' sugar
Choco-mint Filling (right)
1 can Betty Crocker chocolate frosting

Heat oven to 375°

1 Beat eggs in small mixer bowl about 5 minutes or until thick and lemon colored. Gradually beat in granulated sugar. Blend in vanilla and milk on low speed. Gradually add baking mix, beating just until batter is smooth.

2 Pour batter into aluminum foil-lined jelly roll pan, 15½x10½x1 inch, spreading batter to corners.

3 Bake *12 to 15 minutes* or until wooden pick inserted in center comes out clean. Loosen cake from edges of pan; invert on towel sprinkled with confectioners' sugar. Carefully remove foil; trim stiff edges if necessary.

4 While hot, roll cake and towel from narrow end. Cool on wire rack. Unroll cake and remove towel. Spread cake with Choco-mint Filling. Roll up and frost with chocolate frosting, leaving ends unfrosted. With tines of fork, make strokes in frosting to resemble bark. Decorate with red cherries and candy spearmint leaves. Refrigerate. *8 to 12 servings.*

CHOCO-MINT FILLING   Blend ½ can (18-ounce size) Betty Crocker chocolate fudge pudding and ½ teaspoon peppermint extract.

LEPRECHAUN CAKE

Lincoln's Log goes Irish with Grasshopper Filling.

Bake cake as for Lincoln's Log (left). While hot, roll cake and towel from narrow end. Cool on wire rack. Unroll cake and remove towel. Spread cake with Grasshopper Filling (below). Roll up and chill until set, at least 4 hours. Just before serving, sprinkle with confectioners' sugar. *8 to 12 servings.*

GRASSHOPPER FILLING

1½ cups miniature marshmallows
¼ cup milk
2 tbsp green crème de menthe
4 tsp crème de cacao
1 envelope (about 2 oz) dessert
   topping mix

Combine marshmallows and milk in saucepan. Cook over medium heat, stirring constantly, just until marshmallows are melted. Chill until thickened. Blend in liqueurs. Prepare topping mix as directed on package. Fold in marshmallow mixture.

LAMB STEW WITH IRISH DUMPLINGS

Irish or not, shine up the pot and try this delicious dinner-in-a dish with parsley dumplings up top.

2 tbsp shortening
2 lb lamb shoulder, cut into
   2-inch cubes
4 cups water
2 tsp salt
¼ tsp pepper
1 bay leaf
3 medium carrots, cut into
   1-inch slices
1 medium onion, thinly sliced
1 medium potato, pared and cut
   into 1-inch cubes
1 cup peas
2 tbsp Bisquick baking mix
¼ cup water
2 cups Bisquick baking mix
¼ cup snipped parsley
⅔ cup milk

1 Melt shortening in large skillet; brown meat well. Spoon off drippings.

2 Add 4 cups water, the salt, pepper and bay leaf. Heat to boiling; reduce heat. Cover and cook about 2 hours, stirring occasionally.

3 Stir in carrots, onion and potato; cook 20 minutes longer. Stir in peas.

4 Blend 2 tablespoons baking mix and ¼ cup water; stir into stew. Cook over medium heat until mixture thickens and boils.

5 Stir 2 cups baking mix, the parsley and milk to a soft dough. Drop dough by spoonfuls onto boiling stew.

6 Cook uncovered over low heat 10 minutes; cover and cook 10 minutes longer. *6 servings.*

EASTER EGG ROLLS

*Sweet rolls baked in a circle,
frosted and decorated to look
like small Easter egg nests.
Fun for the holiday brunch.*

2⅓ cups Bisquick baking mix
3 tbsp sugar
3 tbsp butter or margarine,
**   melted**
½ cup milk
Creamy Frosting (right)
Colored candies

Heat oven to 450°

1 Stir all ingredients except
frosting and candies to a soft
dough. Gently smooth dough
into a ball on floured cloth-
covered board. Knead 8 to
10 times.

2 Roll dough ½ inch thick. Cut
with floured 2-inch cutter.

3 Arrange biscuits close together
in a circle on ungreased
baking sheet.

4 Bake *8 to 10 minutes* or until
light brown. While warm, frost
with Creamy Frosting and
decorate with candies to
resemble Easter eggs. Serve
immediately. *About 12.*

CREAMY FROSTING Blend
½ cup confectioners' sugar,
1 tablespoon soft butter or
margarine, 2 teaspoons light
cream and ¼ teaspoon
vanilla. If you like, tint with
2 to 3 drops food color.

COLOR YOUR TABLE BOLD
White napkins on a purple
cloth are smashing. Or purple
on purple, napkins and cloth,
accented with stark white
dishes. Or who's to say you
can't combine orange and pink
in napkins and cloth with any
color dishes. Be gay. It's a
holiday brunch.

HOT CROSS BUNS

Traditional yeast bread favorite for brunch or the big dinner itself.

1 pkg active dry yeast
⅔ cup warm water (105 to 115°)
1 egg
¼ cup sugar
2¾ cups Bisquick baking mix
½ tsp cinnamon
¼ tsp nutmeg
½ cup currants
¼ cup chopped citron
Quick Icing (right)

1 Dissolve yeast in warm water in large mixer bowl. Add egg, sugar and 1½ cups of the baking mix.

2 Blend ½ minute on low speed, scraping bowl constantly. Beat 2 minutes medium speed, scraping bowl occasionally.

3 Stir in remaining baking mix, the cinnamon, nutmeg, currants and citron; beat vigorously ½ minute.

4 Spoon dough into 12 greased medium muffin cups. Cover and let rise in warm place until double, about 1 hour.

5 Heat oven to 375°. Bake *15 to 20 minutes* or until golden brown. Make a cross on each bun with Quick Icing. *12 buns.*

QUICK ICING   Blend ½ cup confectioners' sugar and 1 to 2 teaspoons water.

EASTER BRUNCH
Fresh Fruit Cup
Chive Scrambled Eggs
Broiled Tomatoes
Hot Cross Buns
Coffee   Milk

EASTER MONDAY SUPPER BREAD

2 cups Bisquick baking mix
1 cup chopped cooked ham
3 tbsp instant minced onion
2 eggs
⅔ cup milk
2 tbsp salad oil
½ tsp prepared mustard
1½ cups shredded Cheddar cheese (about 6 oz)
2 tbsp sesame seed
3 tbsp butter or margarine, melted

Heat oven to 375°

1 Combine baking mix, ham, onion, eggs, milk, oil, mustard and ¾ cup of the cheese; mix thoroughly.

2 Spread dough in greased 10-inch pie pan. Sprinkle with remaining cheese and the sesame seed. Pour butter evenly over top.

3 Bake *35 to 40 minutes*. Cut into wedges; serve warm. *6 to 8 servings.*

NOTE   Bread can be baked in greased square pan, 9x9x2 inches. Bake in 400° oven 35 to 40 minutes.

RED, WHITE AND BLUE SHORTCAKES

Double berry shortcakes. . .
luscious with strawberries and
blueberries.

2 cups halved fresh strawberries
2 cups blueberries
¼ cup sugar
2⅓ cups Bisquick baking mix
3 tbsp sugar
3 tbsp butter or margarine,
   melted
½ cup milk*
Light cream
Sugar
Whipped cream

Heat oven to 450°

1 Stir together strawberries,
blueberries and ¼ cup sugar;
set aside.

2 Stir baking mix, 3 tablespoons
sugar, the butter and milk to
a soft dough. Gently smooth
dough into a ball on floured
cloth-covered board. Knead
8 to 10 times.

3 Roll dough ½ inch thick. Cut
with floured 3-inch cutter.
Place shortcakes on ungreased
baking sheet. Brush tops with
cream and sprinkle with sugar.

4 Bake *about 10 minutes* or
until light brown.

To serve, split warm
shortcakes; spoon fruit mixture
between halves. Top with
whipped cream. *6 servings.*

*If you like, omit butter and milk and
add ⅔ cup light cream.

SNOWBALLS FOR JULY

For the patio buffet. Do-ahead,
snowy-white cookies. Very
pretty with fresh fruit compote.

⅓ cup butter or margarine,
   softened
½ cup confectioners' sugar
2 cups Bisquick baking mix
½ cup chopped nuts
¾ tsp almond extract
1 to 2 tbsp water
Confectioners' sugar

Heat oven to 350°

1 Cream butter and ½ cup
confectioners' sugar. Stir in
baking mix, nuts and almond
extract. Mix in enough water
to moisten dough.

2 Shape dough by level
teaspoonfuls into balls. Place
on ungreased baking sheet.

3 Bake *about 8 minutes.* Cool
slightly before removing from
baking sheet. While warm, roll
each ball in confectioners'
sugar. *6 dozen.*

APPLE PANCAKES

2 cups Bisquick baking mix
½ tsp cinnamon
1 egg
1⅓ cups milk
¾ cup grated apple

1 Beat baking mix, cinnamon, egg and milk with rotary beater until smooth. Fold in apple.

2 Pour batter from ¼-cup measuring cup onto hot griddle. (Grease griddle if necessary.)

3 Bake until bubbles appear. Turn and bake other side until golden brown. *About 18.*

CIDER SYRUP

1 cup sugar
2 tbsp cornstarch
½ tsp pumpkin pie spice
2 cups apple cider
2 tbsp lemon juice
¼ cup butter or margarine

Mix sugar, cornstarch and spice in saucepan. Stir in cider and juice. Cook, stirring constantly, until mixture thickens and boils 1 minute. Remove from heat and blend in butter.

JACK-O'-LANTERN TEACAKES

Itty-bitty pumpkins — the kind you eat at a spooky party.

2⅓ cups Bisquick baking mix
3 tbsp sugar
3 tbsp butter or margarine, melted
½ cup milk
Orange Frosting (right)
Shoestring licorice
Colored candies

Heat oven to 450°

1 Stir baking mix, sugar, butter and milk to a soft dough. Gently smooth dough into a ball on floured cloth-covered board. Knead 8 to 10 times.

2 Roll dough ¼ inch thick. Cut with floured 2-inch cutter. Form rounds into pumpkin shapes, using extra dough for stems.

3 Bake on ungreased baking sheet *about 8 minutes.* Cool and frost with Orange Frosting. Decorate with licorice and candies to resemble jack-o'-lanterns. *2 dozen.*

ORANGE FROSTING   Blend 1½ cups confectioners' sugar, 1 to 2 tablespoons milk and ½ teaspoon orange extract until of spreading consistency. Reserve 1 tablespoon frosting; color with green food color for stems. Color remainder with red and yellow food color.

PUMPKIN PUFF PANCAKES

For Thanksgiving Day brunch.

2 eggs
1 cup milk
½ cup cooked pumpkin
1¾ cups Bisquick baking mix
2 tbsp sugar
½ tsp *each* cinnamon, nutmeg
   and ginger
¼ cup salad oil

1 Beat eggs in small mixer bowl on high speed 5 minutes or until thick and lemon colored. Stir in remaining ingredients.

2 Pour batter by tablespoonfuls onto medium-hot ungreased griddle.

3 Bake until puffed and bubbles begin to break. Turn and bake other side until golden brown. *About 5 dozen 2-inch pancakes.*

MAPLE RUM-FLAVORED SYRUP   Heat 1 cup maple-flavored syrup and 1 tablespoon butter or margarine. Remove from heat; stir in ½ teaspoon rum flavoring. Serve warm. *About 1 cup.*

CRANBERRY-ORANGE BREAD

Fresh or frozen cranberries can be used. Bread stores well, too, wrapped tightly in aluminum foil.

2½ cups Bisquick baking mix
½ cup sugar
¼ cup Gold Medal flour*
1 egg
1 cup milk
2 tbsp grated orange peel
¾ cup chopped cranberries
½ cup chopped nuts

Heat oven to 350°

1 Combine baking mix, sugar, flour, egg, milk and orange peel; beat vigorously ½ minute. Stir in cranberries and nuts.

2 Pour batter into greased loaf pan, 9x5x3 inches.

3 Bake *1 hour* or until wooden pick inserted in center comes out clean. Cool thoroughly before slicing.

*Do not use self-rising flour in this recipe.

STRICTLY THRIFTY MENUS

You have a food budget that won't behave? Well, join the club. But smile, now — here's where we get shrewd as Scrooge with 16 mini-priced mealtime plots. We rely, of course, on our supper-stretching friend — Bisquick® baking mix. And we offer you hearty main dishes complemented with homey desserts. Hot breads, too, that make pot luck suppers extra special. Plus healthful well-balanced menus on each and every page.

So you can check out all your meals for good nutrition, the Basic Four Food Groups are listed here for your review. Get them down pat. Check the food pages in your daily papers for good buys. Use our ideas to spark your own ingenuity. And I promise you, your strictly thrifty meals can do you proud.

Betty Crocker

Meatball Stew with Egg Dumplings is pictured on the other side of this page. Recipe is on page 28.

FOUR FOR FITNESS

Keep your family happy, healthy and raring to go. Plan your meals around the "basic four" — and serve them every day.

MEATS: 2 or more servings. Including poultry, fish, eggs, dried beans or peas and peanut butter.

VEGETABLES & FRUITS: 4 or more servings. Plan on one dark green or yellow vegetable every other day and one citrus fruit every day.

MILK: 2 or more cups for adults; 3 or 4 cups for children and teenagers. Including cheese and ice cream.

BREADS & CEREALS: 4 or more servings. Make sure they're whole grain, enriched, restored or fortified.

P.S. Don't forget fats, sweets and extra servings from the four groups — they provide additional food energy and other food values.

BUDGET BANQUET

Chicken Fricassee
  with Herb Dumplings
Tossed Salad
Apple Pandowdy
Coffee   Milk

CHICKEN FRICASSEE WITH HERB DUMPLINGS

1 cup Bisquick baking mix
2 tsp salt
1 tsp paprika
⅛ tsp pepper
2½- to 3- lb broiler-fryer chicken,
  cut up
2 tbsp shortening
1 tbsp butter or margarine
1 can (10½ oz) condensed
  cream of chicken soup
1½ cups milk
2 cups Bisquick baking mix
⅔ cup milk
½ tsp parsley flakes
¼ tsp poultry seasoning

1 Blend 1 cup baking mix, the
salt, paprika and pepper;
coat chicken pieces.

2 Cook chicken in shortening
and butter in skillet until light
brown. Remove chicken and
drain fat. Mix soup and 1½
cups milk in skillet; add
chicken pieces.

3 Cover and heat to boiling.
Cook over low heat about
45 minutes or until chicken
is tender.

4 Stir 2 cups baking mix, ⅔ cup
milk, the parsley flakes and
poultry seasoning to a soft
dough. Drop dough by
spoonfuls onto hot soup
mixture.

5 Cook uncovered over low heat
10 minutes; cover and cook
10 minutes longer. *4 servings.*

INVENT A NEW DUMPLING
Omit the parsley flakes and
poultry seasoning and
substitute the following:
¾ cup drained whole kernel
corn and 1 tablespoon
chopped onion. Perfect with
the chicken.

APPLE PANDOWDY

6 apples, pared and cored
2 tbsp water
⅓ cup sugar
1 tsp cinnamon
1 cup Bisquick baking mix
1 tbsp sugar
1 tbsp butter or margarine,
  melted
¼ cup milk

Heat oven to 425°

1 Place apples close together in
greased oblong dish, 10x6x1½
inches, or square pan,
9x9x2 inches. Sprinkle with
water, ⅓ cup sugar and the
cinnamon. Heat in oven 20
minutes while preparing
topping.

2 Stir remaining ingredients
to a soft dough. Gently smooth
dough into a ball on floured
cloth-covered board. Knead
8 to 10 times.

3 Roll dough into a rectangle,
10x6 inches, and place over
hot apples. Cut a small
crisscross in dough on top of
each apple.

4 Bake *20 to 25 minutes.*
6 servings.

SUNDAY DINNER SPECIAL

Oven-fried Chicken
   with Biscuits
Green Peas & Onions
Spinach Salad
Chocolate Sundaes
Coffee   Milk

OVEN-FRIED CHICKEN WITH BISCUITS

World's easiest way to fry chicken — in the oven. Biscuits and peaches baked right along with the chicken.

¼ cup shortening
¼ cup butter or margarine
½ cup Bisquick baking mix
1 tsp salt
1 tsp paprika
¼ tsp pepper
2½ - to 3-lb broiler-fryer chicken, cut up
Whole cloves
1 can (16 oz) peach halves, drained
2 cups Bisquick baking mix
½ cup cold water

Heat oven to 425°

1 Melt shortening and butter in oven in oblong pan, 13x9x2 inches. Blend ½ cup baking mix, the salt, paprika and pepper; coat chicken pieces. Place chicken skin side down in shortening mixture.

2 Bake uncovered *35 minutes.* Insert a clove in each peach.

3 Stir 2 cups baking mix and the water to a soft dough. Gently smooth dough into a ball on floured cloth-covered board. Knead 5 times.

4 Roll dough ½ inch thick. Cut with floured 2-inch cutter.

5 Turn chicken, pushing pieces to one side of pan. Spoon excess fat from pan. Place biscuits in single layer next to chicken. Arrange peach halves on top of chicken.

6 Bake *15 minutes longer* or until biscuits are light brown and chicken is tender. *4 servings.*

NOTE For an easy way to coat chicken, shake several pieces at a time with the Bisquick mixture in paper or plastic bag.

THE TEENAGERS' THING

Chili Casserole
Marinated Green Bean Salad
Milk Shakes
Orange Crunchies

SWINGERS' APPETIZERS

Push the vitamin and protein nibblers: Pineapple and cheese chunks on wooden picks. Peanut butter on celery sticks. Cherry tomatoes in season.

CHILI CASSEROLE

Chili and tomatoes baked under a muffin-like crust, served in soup bowls.

2 cans (15½ oz each) chili with
　beans
1 can (16 oz) tomatoes
1 cup Bisquick baking mix
1 egg
¼ cup milk
1 tsp onion salt
1 tbsp cornmeal

Heat oven to 425°

1 Mix chili and tomatoes in ungreased 2-quart casserole. Heat in oven 10 to 15 minutes while preparing topping.

2 Stir baking mix, egg, milk and onion salt; beat vigorously ½ minute.

3 Spoon batter over hot chili mixture; sprinkle with cornmeal.

4 Bake *25 minutes.* To serve, spoon into soup bowls.
6 servings.

ORANGE CRUNCHIES

Soft drop cookies, chewy with coconut. They store well — if you can keep them around long enough.

2 cups Bisquick baking mix
⅓ cup granulated sugar
⅓ cup brown sugar (packed)
2 tbsp shortening
2 tbsp grated orange peel
¼ cup orange juice
1 egg
1 cup flaked coconut

Heat oven to 400°

1 Blend baking mix, sugars and shortening; mix in remaining ingredients.

2 Drop dough by rounded teaspoonfuls onto greased baking sheet.

3 Bake *about 10 minutes.* Cool slightly before removing from baking sheet. *3 dozen.*

GOOD AS GRAMMA'S

Grilled Franks
Potato Pancakes
Coleslaw
Apricot Jam Cake
Coffee   Milk

MODERN DIVIDENDS

Shortening is even thriftier than cooking with margarine. Dry milk is penny cheap and gives you the same nutrition as skim milk.

POTATO PANCAKES

Crispy old-fashioned pancakes. Sometime try them with hot gravy alongside leftover roast.

¼ cup shortening
2 eggs
¼ cup milk
2 cups finely shredded uncooked
    potatoes, well drained
¼ cup Bisquick baking mix
1 tsp salt

1 Melt shortening in large skillet. Beat eggs with rotary beater until fluffy; stir in remaining ingredients.

2 Drop mixture by tablespoonfuls into hot shortening.

3 Cook about 3 minutes on each side or until golden brown. *About 18 pancakes.*

APRICOT JAM CAKE

No apricot jam? Use peach instead. Serve cake while it's still warm from the oven.

1½ cups Bisquick baking mix
½ cup sugar
1 egg
½ cup milk or water
2 tbsp shortening
1 tsp vanilla
½ cup apricot jam or preserves

Heat oven to 350°

1 Blend all ingredients except jam in large mixer bowl on low speed ½ minute, scraping bowl frequently. Beat 4 minutes medium speed.

2 Pour batter into greased and floured square pan, 8x8x2 inches, or round layer pan, 9x1½ inches.

3 Bake *30 to 35 minutes* or until wooden pick inserted in center comes out clean. While warm, spread with jam.

QUICKLY THRIFTY

Pigs in Blankets
Green Peas & Cheese Salad
Cherry Cobbler
Coffee   Milk

PIGS IN BLANKETS

2 cups Bisquick baking mix
½ cup cold water
12 frankfurters
1 can (16 oz) sauerkraut, well
   drained
Catsup

Heat oven to 450°

1 Stir baking mix and water to a
soft dough. Gently smooth
dough into a ball on floured
cloth-covered board. Knead
5 times.

2 Roll dough into a circle ⅛
inch thick. Cut circle into 12
equal wedges.

3 Spread each wedge with 1
tablespoon sauerkraut. Place
a frankfurter on each wedge;
roll up, beginning at wide end.
Seal tightly by pinching tip
into roll.

4 Bake on ungreased baking
sheet *15 minutes.*

5 Heat remaining sauerkraut;
serve frankfurters with catsup
and hot sauerkraut. *1 dozen.*

CHERRY COBBLER

*Reach for the pie filling —
cherry or another favorite
flavor. Combine with Bisquick
baking mix for a speedy,
luscious cobbler.*

1 can (21 oz) cherry pie filling
1 tbsp grated lemon peel
1 cup Bisquick baking mix
¼ cup butter or margarine,
   softened
3 tbsp bolling water

Heat oven to 400°

1 Mix pie filling and lemon peel
in square pan, 8x8x2 inches.

2 Combine baking mix and
butter in small bowl. Add
water; stir vigorously until
dough forms a ball and cleans
the bowl. (Dough will be puffy
and soft.)

3 Drop dough by spoonfuls onto
fruit mixture.

4 Bake *25 to 30 minutes* or until
topping is golden brown. Serve
warm and, if you like, with
light cream. *9 servings.*

OLD-TIME REVIVAL
Ham Upside-down Casserole
Pickled Beets
Chocolate Pudding
Coffee   Milk

HAM UPSIDE-DOWN CASSEROLE

Smasheroo casserole for leftover ham. Big on nutrition with two vegetables, cheese and a cornmeal bread topping.

1½ cups cubed cooked ham
1 cup drained cooked lima beans
1 can (8 oz) cream-style corn
1 cup shredded sharp Cheddar
  cheese (about 4 oz)
2 tbsp minced onion
1 tsp Worcestershire sauce
⅔ cup Bisquick baking mix
⅓ cup cornmeal
1 egg
¼ cup milk

Heat oven to 400°

1 Mix ham, beans, corn, cheese, onion and Worcestershire sauce. Turn into greased 1½-quart casserole.

2 Cover and bake *15 minutes.*

3 Mix remaining ingredients and spoon over hot meat mixture, spreading batter evenly to edge of casserole.

4 Bake uncovered *20 minutes.* Cut into wedges and invert each onto plate. If you have parsley on hand, use it to garnish. *4 servings.*

CHOCOLATE PUDDING

America's favorite flavor of pudding made in minutes with ingredients off your shelf. Serve in pretty glass dishes.

½ cup Bisquick baking mix
¾ cup sugar
⅓ cup cocoa
1 cup water
2 cups milk

1 Combine baking mix, sugar and cocoa in large saucepan. Gradually stir in water and milk.

2 Cook, stirring constantly, over medium-high heat until mixture thickens and boils. Boil and stir 1 minute.

3 Cool, stirring occasionally. Spoon pudding into serving dishes. *6 servings.*

GOOD OLE STANDBY

Hamburger-Bean Pie
Carrot & Raisin Salad
Peachie Pudding Bake
Coffee   Milk

HAMBURGER-BEAN PIE

Ground beef, green beans and tomato soup baked under a biscuit crust. Hearty and good.

1 lb ground beef
¼ cup chopped onion
1 tsp salt
⅛ tsp pepper
1 can (16 oz) green beans, drained
1 can (10¾ oz) condensed tomato soup
1 cup Bisquick baking mix
¼ cup water

Heat oven to 425°

1 Cook and stir ground beef and onion until meat is brown and onion is tender. Stir in salt, pepper, beans and soup. Heat to boiling, stirring occasionally.

2 Pour mixture into ungreased 1½-quart casserole. Keep hot in oven while preparing topping.

3 Stir baking mix and water to a soft dough. Gently smooth dough into a ball on floured cloth-covered board. Knead 5 times.

4 Roll dough to fit casserole; cut three slits in center. Place dough on hot mixture.

5 Bake *15 minutes. 4 to 6 servings.*

STORING HAMBURGER
Cover loosely and place in coldest part of refrigerator; use within 24 hours. Freeze for longer storage.

PEACHIE PUDDING BAKE

Fresh peaches and brown sugar baked in a pudding, topped with ice cream. Who needs an ice-cream parlor!

8 medium peaches
¾ cup brown sugar (packed) or granulated sugar
1 cup Bisquick baking mix
¼ tsp nutmeg

Heat oven to 425°

1 Peel peaches and slice into large bowl. Sprinkle evenly with sugar and let stand 10 minutes. Stir in baking mix and nutmeg.

2 Turn fruit mixture into greased square pan, 9x9x2 inches.

3 Bake *30 to 35 minutes.* Serve warm and, if you like, with light cream or ice cream. *6 servings.*

LET-'EM-EAT-PIE & CAKE
SUPPER

Hamburger Lattice Pie
Spiced Peaches
Carrot & Celery Sticks
Orange-Nut Cake
Coffee   Milk

HAMBURGER LATTICE PIE

1 lb ground beef
2 tbsp instant minced onion
1 to 2 tsp chili powder
1 tsp oregano
½ tsp garlic salt
¼ tsp pepper
1 egg
1 cup Bisquick baking mix
¼ cup butter or margarine, softened
3 tbsp boiling water

Heat oven to 375°

1 Mix ground beef, onion, chili powder, oregano, garlic salt, pepper and egg. Spread evenly in ungreased 9-inch pie pan.

2 Combine baking mix and butter in small bowl. Add water; stir vigorously until dough forms a ball and cleans the bowl. (Dough will be puffy and soft.)

3 Pat dough with floured hands into 9-inch square on waxed paper. Cut with scissors through waxed paper into 10 strips. Crisscross strips on meat mixture, peeling off paper. Form edge around inside rim with ends of strips.

4 Bake *25 to 30 minutes. 4 to 6 servings.*

ORANGE-NUT CAKE

Orange peel, raisins and nuts in the middle. Goes together in seconds, bakes while you eat.

1½ cups Bisquick baking mix
½ cup brown sugar (packed)
1 egg
½ cup milk or water
2 tbsp grated orange peel
2 tbsp shortening
½ tsp nutmeg
1 tsp vanilla
½ tsp orange extract
½ cup raisins
¼ cup chopped nuts

Heat oven to 350°

1 Blend all ingredients except raisins and nuts in large mixer bowl on low speed ½ minute, scraping bowl frequently. Beat 4 minutes medium speed. Stir in raisins and nuts.

2 Pour batter into greased and floured square pan, 8x8x2 inches.

3 Bake *30 to 35 minutes* or until wooden pick inserted in center comes out clean. If you like, serve warm with whipped topping.

PASTY SUPPER
Tomato Soup
Meat Turnovers
Green Beans
Pear & Cottage Cheese Salad
Fruit Dumplings
Coffee   Milk

MEAT TURNOVERS

Serve with spicy chili sauce. Or heat a can of mushroom soup, undiluted, and add a dash of Worcestershire sauce.

½ lb ground beef
¼ cup chopped onion
2 tbsp Bisquick baking mix
½ tsp salt
¼ tsp monosodium glutamate
¼ tsp garlic salt
½ cup catsup
2 tbsp dairy sour cream
1½ cups Bisquick baking mix
⅓ cup water

Heat oven to 400°

1 Cook and stir ground beef and onion until meat is brown and onion is tender. Stir in 2 tablespoons baking mix, the salt, monosodium glutamate, garlic salt, catsup and sour cream; heat through.

2 Stir 1½ cups baking mix and the water to a soft dough. Gently smooth dough into a ball on floured cloth-covered board. Knead 5 times.

3 Roll dough into a 12-inch square; cut into four 6-inch squares. Place squares on ungreased baking sheet; spoon ⅓ cup meat mixture on each. Fold dough over to make triangles and press edges together to seal securely. Cut slit in center of each turnover.

4 Bake *15 to 20 minutes. 4 servings.*

FRUIT DUMPLINGS

1 tbsp cornstarch
3 tbsp sugar
¼ tsp salt
1 can (17 oz) fruit, drained
   (reserve syrup)
½ tsp grated lemon peel
2 tbsp lemon juice
⅛ tsp cinnamon
1 cup Bisquick baking mix
⅓ cup milk
¼ cup finely chopped nuts

1 Mix cornstarch, sugar and salt in large saucepan. Gradually stir in reserved fruit syrup plus enough water to measure 1½ cups liquid.

2 Cook, stirring constantly, until mixture thickens and boils. Boil and stir 1 minute. Stir in fruit, lemon peel, lemon juice and cinnamon. Keep hot while preparing dumplings.

3 Stir remaining ingredients to a soft dough. Drop dough by 6 spoonfuls onto boiling fruit mixture.

4 Cook uncovered over low heat 10 minutes; cover and cook 10 minutes longer. *6 servings.*

STEW-PENDOUS
PENNYPINCHER

Meatball Stew with Egg
  Dumplings
Lettuce Wedges with French
  Dressing
Coconut Dream Cake
Coffee   Milk

MEATBALL STEW WITH EGG DUMPLINGS

Pictured on chapter cover.

1 lb ground beef
3 tbsp dairy sour cream
¼ cup chopped onion
1 tbsp parsley flakes
1 tsp salt
⅛ tsp pepper
1 can (10½ oz) condensed cream
  of celery soup
3 tbsp dairy sour cream
1 can (16 oz) peas, green beans
  or sliced carrots
1 can (15 oz) potatoes, drained
  and sliced
2 cups Bisquick baking mix
2 eggs
2 tbsp milk

1 Mix ground beef, 3 tablespoons sour cream, the onion, parsley flakes, salt and pepper. Shape mixture into 1-inch balls; brown meatballs on all sides over medium heat in large skillet.

2 Mix soup, 3 tablespoons sour cream, the peas (with liquid) and potatoes; pour over meatballs. Heat to boiling, stirring frequently.

3 Stir remaining ingredients to a soft dough. Drop dough by spoonfuls onto hot mixture.

4 Cook uncovered over low heat 10 minutes; cover and cook 10 minutes longer. *4 to 6 servings.*

COCONUT DREAM CAKE

Simply marvelous warm from the oven. Serve it right from its pan at the table.

1½ cups Bisquick baking mix
½ cup sugar
1 egg
½ cup milk or water
2 tbsp shortening
1 tsp vanilla
½ cup cookie coconut

Heat oven to 350°

1 Blend all ingredients in large mixer bowl on low speed ½ minute, scraping bowl frequently. Beat 4 minutes medium speed.

2 Pour batter into greased and floured square pan, 8x8x2 inches, or round layer pan, 9x1½ inches.

3 Bake *30 to 35 minutes* or until wooden pick inserted in center comes out clean.

DINNER OUT OF A CAN

Hash Pinwheels with
Spunky Cheese Sauce
Whole Green Beans
Fruit Cocktail
Coffee   Milk

HASH PINWHEELS WITH SPUNKY CHEESE SAUCE

*Made like a jelly roll, filled
with hash and served with
your own cheese sauce.*

2 cups Bisquick baking mix
½ cup cold water
2 tbsp shortening
1 can (15 oz) corned beef or
roast beef hash
¼ tsp pepper
Spunky Cheese Sauce (right)

Heat oven to 450°

1 Stir baking mix, water and
shortening to a soft dough.
Gently smooth dough into a
ball on floured cloth-covered
board. Knead 5 times.

2 Roll dough into a rectangle,
12x9 inches. Spread hash over
dough to within ½ inch of
edge; sprinkle with pepper.
Roll up, beginning at narrow
side; cut into nine 1-inch slices.

3 Place slices cut side down in
greased square pan, 9x9x2
inches.

4 Bake *30 minutes* or until
biscuits are golden brown.
Serve hot cheese sauce over
biscuits. *3 or 4 servings.*

SPUNKY CHEESE SAUCE

*The speedy way to make your
own cheese sauce, spunky
with mustard.*

2 tbsp butter or margarine
2 tbsp Bisquick baking mix
¼ tsp salt
¼ tsp dry mustard
⅛ tsp pepper
1 cup milk
½ cup shredded Cheddar cheese

Melt butter over low heat in
saucepan. Blend in baking
mix and seasonings. Cook
over low heat, stirring until
mixture is smooth and bubbly.
Remove from heat and stir in
milk. Heat to boiling, stirring
constantly. Boil and stir
1 minute. Stir in cheese. Heat
over low heat, stirring
constantly, until cheese is
melted. *About 1½ cups.*

NICE ENOUGH FOR COMPANY
Salmon Shortcakes
Buttered Broccoli
Jellied Cucumber Salad
Brownies à la Mode
Coffee   Milk

SALMON SHORTCAKES

2⅓ cups Bisquick baking mix
3 tbsp butter or margarine,
     melted
½ cup milk
1 can (10½ oz) condensed cream
     of mushroom soup
½ cup milk
1 can (16 oz) salmon, drained
¼ cup chopped ripe olives
1 tbsp chopped pimiento
1 tsp parsley flakes
1 tsp Worcestershire sauce

Heat oven to 450°

1 Stir baking mix, butter and ½ cup milk to a soft dough. Gently smooth dough into a ball on floured cloth-covered board. Knead 8 to 10 times.

2 Roll dough ½ inch thick. Cut with floured 3-inch cutter.

3 Bake on ungreased baking sheet *about 10 minutes*.

4 Heat remaining ingredients to boiling over medium heat, stirring frequently.

To serve, split warm shortcakes; spoon salmon mixture between and over halves. *6 servings.*

CHECK THE REFRIGERATOR FOR A CENTERPIECE! Red apples for a wooden bowl. Cucumbers and tomatoes for a basket. Lemons to pop into an apothecary jar.

HOLDOUT TILL PAYDAY

Tuna Casserole with
  Cheese Swirls
Zucchini Slices
Fresh Fruit
  & Chocolate Rounds
Coffee   Milk

TUNA CASSEROLE WITH CHEESE SWIRLS

⅓ cup chopped green pepper
⅓ cup chopped onion
3 tbsp shortening
¼ cup Bisquick baking mix
1 can (10½ oz) condensed cream
  of mushroom or celery soup
1½ cups milk
1 can (6½ oz) tuna, drained
1 can (8½ oz) peas, drained
1 tbsp lemon juice
2 cups Bisquick baking mix
½ cup cold water
¾ cup shredded process
  American cheese

Heat oven to 425°

1 Cook and stir onion and
pepper in shortening in
saucepan until tender. Stir in
¼ cup baking mix. Add soup;
gradually stir in milk. Heat to
boiling over medium heat,
stirring constantly. Boil and
stir 1 minute. Stir in tuna, peas
and lemon juice.

2 Pour mixture into ungreased
baking dish, 11½x7½x1½
inches. Keep hot in oven while
preparing biscuits.

3 Stir 2 cups baking mix and
the water to a soft dough.
Gently smooth dough into a
ball on floured cloth-covered
board. Knead 5 times.

4 Roll dough into a rectangle,
15x9 inches; sprinkle with
cheese. Roll up, beginning at
wide side. Seal well by
pinching edges into dough.
Cut into twelve 1¼-inch slices.
Place slices cut side down
on hot tuna mixture.

5 Bake *20 to 25 minutes.*
4 to 6 servings.

CHOCOLATE ROUNDS

Double chocolate cookies —
both flavored and iced with
chocolate.

½ cup shortening
1 cup sugar
2 eggs
1 tsp vanilla
2 tbsp water
2 squares (1 oz each)
  unsweetened chocolate, melted
2 cups Bisquick baking mix
1 cup chopped nuts
Quick Chocolate Frosting (below)

Heat oven to 350°

1 Mix shortening, sugar, eggs,
vanilla, water and chocolate.
Stir in baking mix and nuts.

2 Drop dough by teaspoonfuls
onto ungreased baking sheet.

3 Bake *15 minutes.* Cool and
frost with Quick Chocolate
Frosting. *About 4 dozen.*

QUICK CHOCOLATE
FROSTING Blend 1 cup
confectioners' sugar, ¼ cup
cocoa and 2 to 3 tablespoons
water.

SOUPER SUPPER

Split Pea Soup
Corn Bread
Cheese & Apple Wedges
Coffee   Milk

CORN BREAD

Scrumptious warm, good reheated. Adds a little soul to any thrifty meal.

1¼ cups Bisquick baking mix
¾ cup cornmeal
2 tbsp sugar
½ tsp salt
1 egg
2 tbsp shortening
⅔ cup milk

Heat oven to 400°

1 Combine all ingredients; beat vigorously ½ minute.

2 Spread batter in greased round layer pan, 9x1½ inches, or square pan, 8x8x2 inches.

3 Bake *20 to 25 minutes.* If you like, brush with butter.
9 to 12 servings.

SALAD SUPPER

Pot Luck Chef's Salad
Quick Onion Bread
Lemon Sherbet
Coffee   Milk

QUICK ONION BREAD

Double-quick, bakes in 10 minutes. Try it with spaghetti, too.

2 cups Bisquick baking mix
½ cup cold water
1 tbsp instant minced onion
1 tbsp soft butter or margarine
Poppy seed

Heat oven to 450°

1 Stir baking mix, water and onion to a soft dough.

2 Roll dough on greased baking sheet into an oblong, 10x8 inches. Spread oblong with butter and sprinkle with poppy seed.

3 Bake *10 minutes.* Serve hot.
6 servings.

SANDWICH SUPPER

Deviled Ham Sandwiches
  on Cheese Biscuits
Omelet   Fruit Cup
Coffee   Milk

CHEESE BISCUITS

Light and tender, with a Cheddar cheese surprise in every bite.

2 cups Bisquick baking mix
½ cup cold water
½ cup shredded Cheddar cheese

Heat oven to 450°

1 Stir all ingredients to a soft dough. Gently smooth dough into a ball on floured cloth-covered board. Knead 5 times.

2 Roll dough ½ inch thick. Cut with floured 2-inch cutter.

3 Bake on ungreased baking sheet *8 to 10 minutes.*
10 to 12 biscuits.

MOBILE MEALS

MOBILE MEALS

Mobile meals are for outdoor fun and games. They go anywhere the action takes you and your family. To the patio or backyard grill, the picnic grounds or the campsite. To the trailer kitchen or the galley on a boat.

And to keep things lively, we offer you some snappy ideas for casual foods: Pizzas and strawberry shortcakes for the outdoor grill. Cheese fondue and flapjacks for campfire cooking. Our favorite Milk Chocolate Brownies for a happy ending to a tailgate party. Quick-energy Candy Dandies for a picnic by snowmobile.

What makes our recipes readily mobile is Bisquick baking mix. It speeds things up for cooking in and carrying out, or it moves right along with you to the outdoor cooking scene. You can take along the recipes, too. They're easy to follow with the new step-by-step directions — even by the light of a campfire.

Remember the rules, now, for mobile meals. Keep hot foods hot and cold foods cold with insulated carriers. And when you come to the end of a perfect cookout, don't forget to douse the fire.

Betty Crocker

Grilled Pizzas are pictured on the preceding page. The recipe is on page 40.

CAMPFIRE CHEESE FONDUE

Fondue fun moves outdoors. Use our do-ahead Breadsticks for dippers. Or peel a long wooden stick, spear a wiener chunk or apple wedge and dunk away.

1 can (10¾ oz) condensed
   Cheddar cheese soup
1 pkg (6 oz) Swiss cheese,
   shredded
Breadsticks (right)

In small saucepan, heat soup and cheese until cheese is melted; stir frequently to prevent sticking. Dip in with Breadsticks. Enjoy! *4 servings.*

BREADSTICKS

Crisp and crunchy for fondue dipping. Bake ahead and carry to the campgrounds.

1 pkg active dry yeast
⅔ cup warm water (105 to 115°)
2½ cups Bisquick baking mix
¼ cup butter or margarine,
   melted
Caraway, poppy, celery or
   sesame seed or garlic salt

1 Dissolve yeast in warm water. Stir in baking mix; beat vigorously.

2 Turn dough onto well-floured board. Knead until smooth, about 20 times. Pour half of the butter into oblong pan, 13x9x2 inches.

3 Divide dough into 16 equal pieces. Roll each between floured hands into pencil-like strips 8 inches long.

4 Place strips in pan. Brush with remaining butter; sprinkle with caraway seed. Cover and let rise in warm place until double, about 1 hour.

5 Heat oven to 425°. Bake *15 minutes* or until light brown. Turn off oven; leave breadsticks in oven 15 minutes. *16 breadsticks.*

OTHER FONDUE DIPPERS
Ham & wiener chunks
Corn chips & crackers
Apple & pear wedges
Cauliflowerets
Cherry tomatoes
Cuke & celery sticks

COFFEE OVER AN OPEN FIRE Heat 2 quarts water to boiling in a 2-pound coffee can (handle with pliers when it's too hot to lift). Dump in 1 cup of regular-grind coffee. Remove coffee can from direct heat and let stand 10 minutes. When you're cooking with eggs, crush the shells and dump them in, too. Pour in ½ cup cold water to settle the grounds. *8 cups.*

WILD BLUEBERRY PANCAKES

Fresh, canned or frozen berries are always good, but it's more fun to pick them wild. Serve pancakes with thick-slice bacon.

2 cups Bisquick baking mix
2 tbsp sugar
1 egg
1⅓ cups milk
1 cup blueberries

1 Beat baking mix, sugar, egg and milk with rotary beater until smooth. Fold in blueberries.

2 Pour batter by spoonfuls onto lightly greased hot skillet.

3 Bake until bubbles appear. Turn and bake other side until golden brown. *About 18.*

LUMBERJACK FLAPJACKS

Made with cornmeal for hearty outdoor eating. You mix the batter and the woodsmen flip their own flapjacks.

1½ cups Bisquick baking mix
1⅓ cups cold water
½ cup cornmeal

1 Beat all ingredients with rotary beater until smooth.

2 Pour batter by spoonfuls onto lightly greased hot skillet.

3 Bake until bubbles appear. Turn and bake other side until golden brown. *About 16.*

CAMPERS' BREAKFAST

Fruit Juice (in serving-size cans)
Lumberjack Flapjacks with Maple Syrup
Brown & Serve Sausages
Coffee   Milk

FRESH AIR FISH FRY

Your master chef can fry the day's catch while you bake up some Skillet Biscuits. Aren't you glad you brought along the Bisquick baking mix?

2 lb pan-dressed fish
1 tsp salt
1/8 tsp pepper
1 egg
1 tbsp water
1 cup Bisquiok baking mix
Shortening (part butter)

1 Sprinkle both sides of fish with salt and pepper. Blend egg and water.

2 Dip fish into egg, then coat with baking mix.

3 Cook fish in hot shortening (1/8 inch deep) over medium heat about 5 minutes on each side. *4 servings.*

SKILLET BISCUITS

1/4 cup butter or margarine
Onion salt, garlic salt and
  paprika
2 cups Bisquick baking mix
1/2 cup cold water

1 Melt butter in 9- or 10-inch skillet. Sprinkle butter with seasonings.

2 Stir baking mix and water to a soft dough. Gently smooth dough into a ball on floured surface. Knead 5 times.

3 Roll or pat dough 1/2 inch thick. Cut with floured 2-inch cutter.

4 Place biscuits in skillet, turning biscuits to coat with seasoned butter. Cover skillet with heavy-duty aluminum foil.

5 Place skillet on grill 4 inches from hot coals; bake 10 minutes. (Lift foil to be sure biscuits are not burning.) Bake 5 minutes longer or until biscuits are done. *10 biscuits.*

CINNAMON-SUGAR BALLS

Do-it-yourself campfire bread. For a breakfast dessert or supper sweet.

1/4 cup butter or margarine
1/3 cup sugar
1 tsp cinnamon
1 cup Bisquick baking mix
1/4 cup cold water

1 Melt butter in small pan on grill. Mix sugar and cinnamon; set aside.

2 Stir baking mix and water to a soft dough.

3 Shape dough into 1-inch balls around peeled ends of green sticks; secure dough by pressing gently.

4 Cook over campfire 5 minutes, rotating slowly, until evenly browned. Roll biscuits in butter, then in sugar mixture. *1 dozen.*

CAMP TRAIL CORN BREAD

Ever see appetites go wild? Watch — when you bake corn bread outdoors in a reflector oven.

1¼ cups Bisquick baking mix
¾ cup cornmeal
2 tbsp sugar
1 egg
⅔ cup cold water

1 Mix all ingredients; beat vigorously ½ minute.
2 Pour batter into hot greased square pan, 8x8x2 inches.
3 Bake in hot reflector oven 15 minutes; turn pan and bake 10 to 15 minutes longer or until golden brown. *6 to 8 servings.*

HOT DROP BISCUITS

Out-of-doors, out of this world, baked in a portable oven.

2 cups Bisquick baking mix
½ cup cold water

1 Stir ingredients to a soft dough.
2 Drop dough by spoonfuls onto greased shiny side of heavy-duty aluminum foil.
3 Bake in hot reflector oven about 15 minutes or until golden brown. *10 biscuits.*

SWEET CINNAMON ROLLS
Mix 2 tablespoons sugar and 1 teaspoon cinnamon in small bag. Drop one spoonful of dough at a time into sugar mixture; shake to coat thoroughly.

CAMPERS' SANDWICHES

2 cups Bisquick baking mix
⅓ cup cold water
¼ cup butter or margarine, melted
Eight ⅛-inch slices pork luncheon meat
⅓ cup chili sauce or pickle relish

1 Stir baking mix, water and butter to a soft dough.
2 Divide dough into 8 equal parts; place each part on sheet of waxed paper. With floured hands, pat each into a 5-inch square.
3 Top half of each square with meat slice; spread each with about 2 teaspoons chili sauce. Fold dough over meat; press edges with fork to seal securely. Make slit on top of each.
4 Place on greased dull side of heavy-duty aluminum foil. Bake in hot reflector oven 25 to 30 minutes or until golden brown. *4 servings.*

BARBECUE BEEFBURGERS

1 lb ground beef
2 tbsp chopped onion
1 tsp salt
¼ tsp pepper
Bottled barbecue sauce
1½ cups Bisquick baking mix
⅓ cup cold water

1 Mix meat, onion, salt and pepper; shape mixture into 4 patties.

2 Place patties on grill about 4 inches from hot coals; cook about 10 minutes on each side, brushing occasionally with barbecue sauce.

3 Stir baking mix and water to a soft dough. Divide dough into 8 equal parts. With floured hands, flatten each part to size of beef patty.

4 Place biscuits on grill about 4 inches from hot coals; cook 2 to 3 minutes on each side or until golden brown.
To serve, place a meat patty between 2 biscuits. *4 servings.*

HOBO DINNERS-IN-CANS

1 lb ground beef
4 tomatoes, sliced
1 can (17 oz) whole kernel corn, drained
Salt and pepper
Butter or margarine
1 cup Bisquick baking mix
⅓ cup milk

1 Divide meat into 4 patties. Place a meat patty in each of 4 lightly greased 1-pound coffee cans.

2 Top each patty with 3 tomato slices and ¼ of the corn. Season with salt and pepper; dot with butter. Cover each can tightly with heavy-duty aluminum foil.

3 Place cans on grill 3 to 4 inches from hot coals; cook 20 to 30 minutes.

4 Stir baking mix and milk to a soft dough. Drop dough by spoonfuls into each can.

5 Cook uncovered 10 minutes; cover and cook 10 minutes longer. *4 servings.*

GRILLED PIZZAS

Pictured on chapter cover.

2 cups Bisquick baking mix
½ tsp salt
½ cup cold water
1 bottle (14 oz) catsup
1 pkg (3½ oz) sliced **pepperoni**
2 pkg (4 oz each) shredded
   mozzarella cheese
Oregano leaves

1 Stir baking mix, salt and water to a soft dough. Gently smooth dough into a ball on floured surface. Knead 5 times.

2 Divide dough into 4 equal parts. Roll or pat each part into an 8-inch circle.

3 Place circles on grill 5 inches from medium coals; cook 8 minutes.

4 Turn and spread with catsup. Top with pepperoni and cheese; sprinkle with oregano.

5 Cook 12 to 15 minutes longer or until edges are brown.
4 servings.

ZEBRA BREAD

Cracker-like bread with sesame flavor. Baked right on the grill for striped effect. Good with ribs or chicken.

2 cups Bisquick baking mix
¼ cup sesame seed
½ tsp salt
½ cup cold water
Butter or margarine

1 Stir baking mix, sesame seed, salt and water to a soft dough. Gently smooth dough into a ball on floured surface. Knead 5 times.

2 Divide dough in half. Roll or pat each half into a rectangle, 12x8 inches; cut lengthwise in half.

3 Place strips on grill 5 inches from medium coals; cook 3 to 4 minutes on each side. Cut each strip into 4 pieces and serve hot with butter.
16 pieces.

ONION BUTTER BISCUITS

Crispy, oniony drop biscuits for a steak fry.

⅓ cup butter or margarine
¼ cup onion soup mix
2 cups Bisquick baking mix
½ cup cold water

1 Melt butter in 8-inch foil pie pan on grill; stir in 2 tablespoons of the soup mix. Pour half the butter mixture into another 8-inch foil pie pan. Rotate pans until butter mixture covers bottoms and sides.

2 Stir baking mix, remaining soup mix and the water to a soft dough. Drop dough by spoonfuls into hot butter mixture. Pour butter mixture from other pan over biscuits; invert pan over pan with biscuits. Secure rims together with spring-type clothespins.

3 Place pan on grill 4 inches from hot coals; cook 8 to 10 minutes on each side. *Ten 2-inch biscuits.*

BIG DADDY GRILLED SHORTCAKE

Clothespinned foil pans turn your grill into an oven for baking one large shortcake at the campsite.

2⅓ cups Bisquick baking mix
3 tbsp sugar
3 tbsp butter or margarine, melted
½ cup milk
Fresh strawberries

1 Stir baking mix, sugar, butter and milk to a soft dough.

2 Spread dough in one greased 9-inch foil pie pan. Invert another greased 9-inch foil pie pan over pan with dough. Secure rims together with spring-type clothespins.

3 Place on grill 4 inches from hot coals. Cook 15 minutes on each side or until brown. Serve warm with strawberries. *6 to 8 servings.*

SERVING-SIZE SHORTCAKES

Here's another twist for outdoor shortcakes. This time they're biscuit-size shortcakes, baked ahead and brought to the outdoor grill for reheating in foil packets. Bake up a batch of Regular Shortcakes with Bisquick baking mix, then proceed as follows.

Split baked shortcakes and butter lightly. Wrap each shortcake tightly in 9x7-inch piece of heavy-duty aluminum foil. Place shortcakes on grill 3 to 4 inches from hot coals; heat 5 minutes on each side. Open foil packets and shape into plates. Spoon fruit between and over layers and feast away. *6 servings.*

MINI-SUB SANDWICHES

Fun for a party on the patio. Double deck ham-and-cheese sandwiches — on poppy seed buns baked in custard cups.

4 cups Bisquick baking mix
1 envelope (1½ oz) sour cream
  sauce mix
1¾ cups milk
2 eggs
Poppy seed
2 pkg (3 oz each) cream
  cheese, softened
1 tbsp brown sugar
1 tsp grated orange peel
2 tbsp orange juice
12 thin slices cooked ham
1 pkg (8 oz) sliced Swiss cheese
Lettuce leaves

Heat oven to 400°

1 Combine baking mix, sauce mix, milk and eggs; beat vigorously ½ minute.

2 Spread batter in six greased 10-ounce custard cups. Sprinkle with poppy seed.

3 Bake *about 20 minutes.* Cool. Slice each round horizontally into thirds.

4 Blend cream cheese, sugar, orange peel and juice. Spread cut sides of bread with cream cheese mixture.

5 Fill layers with ham and cheese slices and lettuce; secure with wooden picks.
6 sandwiches.

PATIO PARTY

Mini-Sub Sandwiches
Fruit Kabobs
Velvet Fudge Cake
Crème de Menthe Ice-Cream
  Sodas

VELVET FUDGE CAKE

1½ cups Bisquick baking mix
⅓ cup sugar
1 egg
½ cup milk or water
½ cup semisweet chocolate
  pieces, melted and cooled
2 tbsp shortening
1 tsp vanilla
Chocolate-Coconut Frosting
  (below)

Heat oven to 350°

1 Blend all ingredients except frosting in large mixer bowl on low speed ½ minute, scraping bowl frequently. Beat 4 minutes medium speed.

2 Pour batter into greased and floured square pan, 8x8x2 inches.

3 Bake *30 to 35 minutes* or until wooden pick inserted in center comes out clean. Cool and frost.

CHOCOLATE-COCONUT
FROSTING Mix ½ cup semisweet chocolate pieces, melted, 1 can (3½ ounces) flaked coconut and ¼ cup water.

SOUR CREAM COFFEE CAKE

Delicious surprise for brunch outside.

1½ cups Bisquick baking mix
½ cup sugar
2 tbsp butter or margarine, softened
1 egg
¾ cup dairy sour cream
1 tsp vanilla
Topping (below)

Heat oven to 350°

1 Combine all ingredients except Topping; beat vigorously 1 minute.

2 Spread batter in greased square pan, 8x8x2 inches. Sprinkle with Topping.

3 Bake *35 minutes.* Serve warm. *9 servings.*

TOPPING Mix ¼ cup Gold Medal flour, 3 tablespoons sugar, ⅛ teaspoon cinnamon and 2 tablespoons firm butter or margarine until crumbly.

CRISPY CHEESE TWISTS

Dainty cheese rolls. Pretty with shrimp salad for a ladies' luncheon on the patio.

1 cup Bisquick baking mix
¼ cup cold water
¼ cup butter or margarine, softened
⅓ cup shredded process American cheese

Heat oven to 450°

1 Stir baking mix and water to a soft dough.

2 Roll dough into a rectangle, 12x10 inches, on greased aluminum foil-covered baking sheet. Spread rectangle with butter and sprinkle with cheese.

3 Fold dough lengthwise in half; pinch edges to seal securely. Cut into ¾-inch strips. Gently twist each strip and place on foil-covered baking sheet.

4 Bake *6 to 8 minutes.* Serve immediately. *16 twists.*

BANANA-APRICOT NUT BREAD

Spread with cream cheese, serve with iced coffee. In the garden.

3 cups Bisquick baking mix
⅔ cup sugar
⅓ cup Gold Medal flour
1 egg
½ cup milk
1 cup mashed bananas (2 to 3 medium)
½ cup chopped nuts
½ cup cut-up dried apricots

Heat oven to 350°

1 Combine baking mix, sugar, flour, egg, milk and bananas; beat vigorously ½ minute. Stir in nuts and apricots.

2 Pour batter into greased loaf pan, 9x5x3 inches.

3 Bake *50 to 60 minutes* or until wooden pick inserted in center comes out clean. Cool thoroughly before slicing.

FRUIT FIESTA PIE

A summer's fiesta of fruit on a short crust pie shell that's baked in a pizza pan. For a fancy party on the patio.

2 cups Bisquick baking mix
2 pkg (3 oz each) cream cheese, softened
¼ cup butter or margarine, softened

Heat oven to 425°

1 Mix all ingredients in bowl; work with hands until dough forms a ball and cleans the bowl.

2 Roll dough to a 14-inch circle on lightly floured cloth-covered board. Ease into 13-inch pizza pan; flute edge. Chill 10 minutes.

3 Bake *8 to 10 minutes* or until light brown. Cool.

FILLING & SAUCE

Clear Orange Sauce (below)
1 pt fresh strawberries, halved
3 fresh peaches, peeled and sliced
1½ cups seedless green grapes
2 tbsp sugar

Prepare Clear Orange Sauce. Cool. Arrange fruits in circles in pastry shell; sprinkle with sugar. Spoon some of the sauce over fruits. Cut pie into wedges; serve with remaining sauce. *10 to 12 servings.*

CLEAR ORANGE SAUCE

Mix 1 cup sugar, ¼ teaspoon salt and 2 tablespoons cornstarch in small saucepan. Stir in 1 cup orange juice, ¼ cup lemon juice and ¾ cup water. Cook, stirring constantly, until mixture thickens and boils. Boil and stir 1 minute. Remove from heat. Stir in ½ teaspoon *each* grated orange and lemon peel.

SUMMER SPREE

Rotisserie Turkey
Corn on the Cob
Caesar's Salad
Fruit Fiesta Pie
Iced Tea

TWO IN A CANOE

Salami
Cheese Bread
Apples
Wine

GALLEY HOSPITALITY

Corned Beef
Breads in the Round
Mustard   Dill Pickles
Candy Dandies (page 47)
Hot Coffee

CHEESE BREAD

*Delicious hot or cold. For a
picnic in a canoe, wrap in
foil and carry along a cutting
knife.*

1 egg
1½ cups milk
3¾ cups Bisquick baking mix
1 cup shredded natural sharp
   Cheddar cheese (about 4 oz)

Heat oven to 350°

1 Beat egg on low speed. Add
   remaining ingredients and
   beat ½ minute medium speed
   until blended.
2 Pour batter into greased loaf
   pan, 9x5x3 inches.
3 Bake *1 hour* or until golden
   brown.

BREADS IN THE ROUND

*No oven in the galley? Bake at
home — one little loaf per
person. Let the crew slice and
make their own sandwiches.*

4 cups Bisquick baking mix
1 envelope (1½ oz) sour cream
   sauce mix
2 tbsp snipped chives
2 eggs
1¾ cups milk
Sesame seed

Heat oven to 400°

1 Mix all ingredients except
   sesame seed; beat vigorously
   ½ minute.
2 Spread batter in six greased
   10-ounce custard cups.
   Sprinkle with sesame seed.
3 Bake *about 20 minutes.
   6 rounds.*

PICNIC ON THE PORCH

Beef Fondue
Horseradish & Barbecue
  Sauces
Tossed Green Salad
Dill Snack Buns
Fresh Peaches
Spiced Coffee

4TH OF JULY PICNIC

Cheesy Pups
Potato Salad
Crisp Relishes
S'mores
Cold Beer & Pop

DILL SNACK BUNS

Tiny yeast breads to serve with beef fondue at a picnic on the porch.

1 pkg active dry yeast
⅔ cup warm water (105 to 115°)
2½ cups Bisquick baking mix
2 tsp dill weed
Soft butter or margarine

1 Dissolve yeast in warm water. Stir in baking mix and dill weed; beat vigorously.

2 Turn dough onto floured board. Knead until smooth, about 20 times.

3 Divide dough into 32 equal pieces; shape into balls.

4 Place balls in greased round layer pan, 8x1½ inches. Cover and let rise in warm place until double, about 1 hour.

5 Heat oven to 400°. Bake *15 to 20 minutes* or until light brown. Brush with butter. *32 buns.*

CHEESY PUPS

Fourth of July favorite. The all-American hot dog, grilled in a blanket of cheese dough that's wrapped with a strip of bacon.

2 cups Bisquick baking mix
½ cup shredded Cheddar
  cheese
½ cup cold water
10 frankfurters
10 bacon slices

1 Stir baking mix, cheese and water to a soft dough. Divide dough into 10 equal pieces.

2 Pat each piece of dough around a frankfurter, making a thin coating. Wrap a bacon slice around dough, securing ends with wooden picks.

3 Place on grill 4 inches from hot coals; cook, turning frequently, 15 minutes or until bacon is crisp and biscuit cooked. *5 servings.*

PICNIC BY SNOWMOBILE

Ham Sandwiches
Candy Dandies
Hot Mulled Cider

CANDY DANDIES

*Candy bar cookies chewy
with coconut, chocolate and
nuts. Good for quick energy
at a picnic in the snow.*

¼ cup butter or margarine,
　softened
¾ cup brown sugar (packed)
1 egg
1½ cups Bisquick baking mix
½ cup chopped nuts
2 bars (about 1½ oz each)
　chocolate-covered coconut or
　almond candy, cut up

Heat oven to 375°

1 Mix butter, sugar and egg;
　stir in remaining ingredients.

2 Drop dough by teaspoonfuls
　2 inches apart onto ungreased
　baking sheet.

3 Bake *about 10 minutes* or
　until light brown. *About
　3 dozen.*

BIKERS' PICNIC

Summer Sausage Sandwiches
Chocolate Chip Cookies
Oranges

CHOCOLATE CHIP COOKIES

½ cup butter or margarine,
　softened
1 cup brown sugar (packed)
1 egg
2 cups Bisquick baking mix
½ cup chopped nuts
1 pkg (6 oz) semisweet
　chocolate pieces

Heat oven to 375°

1 Mix butter, sugar and egg;
　stir in remaining ingredients.

2 Drop dough by rounded
　teaspoonfuls 2 inches apart
　onto ungreased baking sheet.

3 Bake *about 10 minutes* or
　until light brown. *About 4
　dozen.*

TAILGATE PARTY

Hot Tomato Juice
Hibachi Kabobs
Three-Bean Salad
Cantaloupe Wedges &
    Milk Chocolate Brownies
Coffee

For Hibachi Kabobs, lamb is the classic choice — plus cherry tomatoes, mushrooms, pineapple chunks and green pepper pieces. Marinate the lamb cubes a couple hours in bottled French dressing. Store everything in a cooler to travel.

TRAILER KITCHEN PICNIC

Super Sloppy Joe
Potato Chips
Cherry Tomatoes
Dill Pickles
Chocolate Chip Cookies
    (page 47)
Coffee   Milk

MILK CHOCOLATE BROWNIES

Brownies are always great at a tailgate party, but these are extra special with chocolate chips and nuts in every bite.

1 pkg (6 oz) semisweet
    chocolate pieces
1 can (14 oz) sweetened
    condensed milk
2 tbsp salad oil
1 cup chopped nuts
2 cups Bisquick baking mix

Heat oven to 375°

1 Melt chocolate pieces over low heat. Combine milk, oil and nuts in large bowl; stir in chocolate and baking mix.

2 Spread dough in greased oblong pan, 13x9x2 inches.

3 Bake *about 20 minutes.* Cool slightly and cut into 1½-inch squares. *4 dozen.*

SUPER SLOPPY JOE

Cooking in a trailer kitchen that has an oven? Here's a giant-size Sloppy Joe with barbecue beef baked in the middle. Cut and serve picnic-style on paper plates.

2 cups Bisquick baking mix
⅔ cup milk
¼ cup mayonnaise or salad
    dressing
1 can (15½ oz) barbecue sauce
    and beef
Paprika

Heat oven to 400°

1 Stir baking mix and milk; blend in mayonnaise.

2 Spread half the mixture in greased square pan, 8x8x2 inches. Cover with beef mixture. Drop remaining dough by spoonfuls over beef mixture and spread evenly. Sprinkle with paprika.

3 Bake *35 minutes.* Cut into squares. *8 servings.*

BE-MY-GUEST BEST

BE MY GUEST

Like to get a little audience reaction at your parties? These are the foods that can do it. Appetizers, casual for snacktime and sophisticated for the cocktail hour. Fancy breads for brunch and sitdown dinners. Elegant entrees for daylight and candlelight. Glamorous desserts that can stage parties by themselves. All of these recipes are so beautifully simplified with Bisquick baking mix, they make partytime fun for the hostess, too.

Now, about the party table. Do be daring with color: Splashy prints are gay for brunch. Polka dot vinyl is grand for cutting out runners or place mats for buffet service. Cloths of solid colors are dramatic for candlelight suppers. To show off pretty napkins, flip them loose and stuff into empty water goblets. And if you're going to open a bottle of wine, remember — red wines at cool room temperature, white and rosé wines well chilled. And pour the glasses just half full.

Enough for preliminaries. Get on the phone and call your friends, and have a lovely party.

Betty Crocker

See our table setting for Butterfly Shrimp on the preceding page. The recipe is on page 59.

BURGER BOATS

1 lb ground beef
⅓ cup chopped onion
½ tsp salt
⅛ tsp pepper
¼ cup chili sauce
¼ cup sweet pickle relish
2⅓ cups Bisquick baking mix
3 tbsp butter or margarine,
   melted
½ cup milk

Heat oven to 400°

1 Mix ground beef, onion, salt,
  pepper, chili sauce and
  pickle relish; set aside.

2 Stir remaining ingredients
  to a soft dough. Gently smooth
  dough into a ball on floured
  cloth-covered board. Knead
  8 to 10 times.

3 Roll dough into a rectangle,
  15x9 inches; cut into fifteen
  3-inch squares. Place on
  ungreased baking sheet;
  spoon meat mixture on each.
  Fold sides up and pinch ends
  together to form boats.

4 Bake *20 to 25 minutes* or
  until light brown. *15 appetizers.*

PEPPERONI SQUARES

2 cups Bisquick baking mix
2 hard-cooked eggs, chopped
½ cup chopped pepperoni
2 tbsp instant minced onion
   or ½ cup chopped onion
1 tsp oregano leaves
⅛ tsp pepper
⅔ cup milk
Soft butter or margarine

Heat oven to 450°

1 Mix all ingredients except
  butter.

2 Spread dough in greased
  square pan, 9x9x2 inches.
  Brush with butter.

3 Bake *15 to 20 minutes.* Cut
  into squares. Serve warm.
  9 to 12 servings.

SNACKTIME SOCIABILITY
Serve any of these appetizers
as finger foods. Or turn them
into casual suppers with
mushroom, cheese or tomato
sauce. Mugs of beer, cola or
cider for beverage.

TUNA SNACKS

1 can (6½ oz) tuna, drained
¼ cup sweet pickle relish
½ tsp salt
1 tbsp prepared mustard
3 tbsp mayonnaise or salad
   dressing
2 cups Bisquick baking mix
½ cup cold water

Heat oven to 450°

1 Mix tuna, relish, salt, mustard
  and mayonnaise; set aside.

2 Stir baking mix and water
  to a soft dough. Divide in half.

3 Roll one half into a 9-inch
  square on greased baking
  sheet.

4 Spread tuna mixture over
  square. Roll other half of
  dough into 9-inch square;
  place over tuna mixture.

5 Bake *10 to 12 minutes.* Cut
  into squares. Serve warm.
  3 dozen.

CHEESE HORS D'OEUVRES

For the cocktail hour or a wine-tasting party. Tender little cheese balls wrapped in a coat of parsley and onion. Good hot or cold.

½ cup snipped parsley or chives
1 tbsp minced onion
1 cup Bisquick baking mix
½ cup shredded process sharp
　Cheddar cheese
2 tbsp mayonnaise or salad
　dressing
¼ cup cold water

Heat oven to 450°

1 Mix parsley and onion; set aside. Stir remaining ingredients to a soft dough.

2 Shape dough into 1-inch balls and roll in parsley mixture.

3 Bake on greased baking sheet *about 7 minutes. About 24.*

Picture at right shows both Cheese Hors d'oeuvres and Devilish Canapés.

DEVILISH CANAPÉS

Ham spread on sour cream biscuit rounds. Sixty of them.

2 cups Bisquick baking mix
⅓ cup butter or margarine,
　softened
1 pkg (8 oz) cream cheese,
　softened
1 envelope (2½ oz) sour cream
　sauce mix
1 tsp dill weed
Deviled Ham Spread (right)

Heat oven to 450°

1 Blend baking mix, butter, cream cheese and sauce mix; work with hands to form a soft dough.

2 Divide dough in half. Roll each half about ⅛ inch thick on floured board. Cut with floured 2-inch cutter; sprinkle with dill weed.

3 Bake on ungreased baking sheet *about 5 minutes* or until light brown. Cool. Spread each appetizer with about ½ teaspoon Deviled Ham Spread. *About 5 dozen.*

DEVILED HAM SPREAD

1 can (4½ oz) deviled ham
¼ cup mayonnaise or salad
　dressing
2 tbsp snipped parsley
2 tbsp minced onion
4 drops red pepper sauce

Mix all ingredients.

BANANA MUFFS

Tiny frosted muffins. Pretty with a fresh fruit plate for an all-girl brunch.

2 cups Bisquick baking mix
¼ cup sugar
2 tbsp butter or margarine, softened
1 egg
1 cup mashed ripe bananas (2 to 3 medium)
Thin Icing (below)
Chopped nuts

Heat oven to 400°

1 Combine baking mix, sugar, butter and egg; beat vigorously ½ minute. Fold in bananas.

2 Fill 48 greased tiny muffin cups ⅔ full.

3 Bake *12 to 15 minutes.* While warm, frost with Thin Icing and sprinkle with nuts.
4 dozen.

THIN ICING   Blend ½ cup confectioners' sugar and 1 tablespoon water.

NUTTY LITTLE LOAVES

3 cups Bisquick baking mix
½ cup sugar
⅓ cup Gold Medal flour
1 egg
1 cup milk
1½ cups chopped nuts

Heat oven to 350°

1 Combine baking mix, sugar, flour, egg and milk; beat vigorously ½ minute. Stir in nuts.

2 Pour batter into 6 well-greased miniature loaf pans, 4½ x 2¾ x 1¼ inches.

3 Bake *about 35 minutes* or until wooden pick inserted in center comes out clean. Cool thoroughly before slicing.

LITTLE ROUNDS   Pour batter into 5 well-greased 10½-ounce soup cans or 8 well-greased 6-ounce aluminum juice cans. Bake soup cans *about 40 minutes,* juice cans *about 35 minutes.*

BUTTERSCOTCH PECAN RING

Scrumptious for a party brunch. Ever try chicken livers with curried rice?

⅓ cup butter or margarine
⅓ cup brown sugar (packed)
Drained maraschino cherries
Pecan halves
2 cups Bisquick baking mix
2 tbsp granulated sugar
1 egg
⅔ cup water or milk

Heat oven to 400°

1 Melt butter in oven in 6½-cup ring mold. Sprinkle evenly with brown sugar. Arrange cherries and pecans over sugar mixture.

2 Mix remaining ingredients; beat vigorously ½ minute.

3 Spoon batter evenly over cherries and pecans.

4 Bake *25 to 30 minutes.* Invert onto heatproof plate. Leave pan over coffee cake a few minutes. Serve warm.
9 to 12 servings.

GOURMET DINNER ROLLS

Yeast breads, fancy cut and flavored with Parmesan cheese and garlic. Perfect with roast beef or Stroganoff.

1 pkg active dry yeast
⅔ cup warm water (105 to 115°)
2½ cups Bisquick baking mix
1 tbsp soft butter or margarine
2 tbsp grated Parmesan cheese
1 tsp garlic powder

1 Dissolve yeast in warm water. Stir in baking mix; beat vigorously.

2 Turn dough onto floured board. Knead until smooth, about 20 times.

3 Roll dough into a rectangle, 12x9 inches. Spread with butter; sprinkle with cheese and garlic powder.

4 Cut into twelve 3-inch squares. Roll up each as for jelly roll; place seam side down on greased baking sheet. Make cuts halfway through dough at ½-inch intervals. Curve slightly to separate cuts.

5 Cover and let rise in warm place until double, about 30 minutes.

6 Heat oven to 400°. Bake *10 to 15 minutes* or until golden brown. *1 dozen.*

BISCUIT FAN-TANS

Something new in fan-tans. Two buttery biscuits baked together in a muffin cup. Serve with wine or herb jelly for your most elegant dinner party.

2 cups Bisquick baking mix
½ cup cold water
¼ cup soft butter or margarine

Heat oven to 450°

1 Stir baking mix and water to a soft dough. Gently smooth dough into a ball on floured cloth-covered board. Knead 5 times.

2 Roll dough ¼ inch thick. Spread half of the butter over half of the dough; fold over and spread remaining butter over half of the dough. Fold in half and roll ½ inch thick. Cut with floured 2-inch cutter. Place 2 biscuits cut sides up in each ungreased muffin cup.

3 Bake *about 10 minutes. 8 or 9 biscuits.*

WAIKIKI UPSIDE DOWN CAKE

Our fanciest version of the pineapple upside-down cake. Serve on a cake platter decorated with a lei of tiny flowers.

2 tbsp butter or margarine
¼ cup brown sugar (packed)
1 can (8½ oz) sliced pineapple, drained
1½ cups Bisquick baking mix
½ cup granulated sugar
1 egg
½ cup milk or water
2 tbsp shortening
1 tsp vanilla
½ cup cookie coconut

Heat oven to 350°

1 Melt butter in oven in square pan, 8x8x2 inches, or round layer pan, 9x1½ inches. Sprinkle with brown sugar; arrange pineapple slices on brown sugar.

2 Blend remaining ingredients in large mixer bowl on low speed ½ minute, scraping bowl frequently. Beat 4 minutes medium speed.

3 Pour batter over butter mixture and pineapple slices.

4 Bake *30 to 35 minutes* or until wooden pick inserted in center comes out clean. Invert onto heatproof plate. Leave pan over cake a few minutes. Serve warm.

HAWAIIAN DINNER PARTY

Rum Punch
Macadamia Nuts
Sweet & Sour Pork
White Rice
Green Cabbage Salad
Waikiki Upside-down Cake
Coffee Tea

JUBILEE CHERRY TOP-OVER

1 can (21 oz) cherry pie filling
1½ cups Bisquick baking mix
½ cup sugar
1 egg
½ cup milk or water
2 tbsp shortening
1 tsp vanilla
Whipped cream

Heat oven to 350°

1 Spread pie filling in ungreased square pan, 9x9x2 inches. Heat in oven 15 minutes.

2 Blend remaining ingredients except whipped cream in large mixer bowl on low speed ½ minute, scraping bowl frequently. Beat 4 minutes medium speed.

3 Pour batter over hot pie filling.

4 Bake *45 to 50 minutes* or until wooden pick inserted in center comes out clean. Invert onto heatproof plate. Leave pan over cake a few minutes. Serve warm with whipped cream.

HAPPY BIRTHDAY CAKE

A two-layer beauty iced with our fluffy white frosting. For a swinger's birthday, decorate with a mod daisy. See how easy it is to do at the right.

3 cups Bisquick baking mix
1 cup sugar
2 eggs
1 cup milk or water
¼ cup shortening
2 tsp vanilla
1 pkg Betty Crocker fluffy white
**   frosting mix**

Heat oven to 350°

1 Blend all ingredients except frosting in large mixer bowl on low speed ½ minute, scraping bowl frequently. Beat 4 minutes medium speed.

2 Pour batter into 2 greased and floured round layer pans, 9x1½ inches.

3 Bake *30 to 35 minutes* or until wooden pick inserted in center comes out clean. Cool; remove from pans. Prepare frosting mix as directed on package; fill layers and frost cake.

FROSTING ARTISTICS
To outline daisy, use Betty Crocker canned vanilla frosting colored with black paste food color in a decorators' tube. Or form the outline with shoestring licorice. Then fill in design with colored candies.

CHOCOLATE CHIP CAKE

Chocolate peppermint wafers inside and out. With candles, it's a child's birthday cake.

1½ cups Bisquick baking mix
½ cup sugar
1 egg
½ cup milk or water
2 tbsp shortening
1 tsp vanilla
13 chocolate peppermint candy
**   wafers, finely chopped (⅓ cup)**
15 to 20 chocolate peppermint
**   candy wafers**

Heat oven to 350°

1 Blend all ingredients except wafers in large mixer bowl on low speed ½ minute, scraping bowl frequently. Beat 4 minutes medium speed. Fold in chopped wafers.

2 Pour batter into greased and floured round layer pan, 9x1½ inches.

3 Bake *about 35 minutes*. Place wafers on hot cake; when softened, spread evenly over top.

ALMOND BUTTERBALLS

⅓ cup sugar
⅓ cup finely chopped nuts
1¼ cups Bisquick baking mix
¼ cup butter or margarine, softened
½ tsp vanilla
½ tsp almond extract
3 tbsp boiling water
1 egg white, slightly beaten

Heat oven to 375°

1 Mix sugar and nuts; set aside.

2 Combine baking mix, butter and flavorings in small bowl. Add water; stir vigorously until dough forms a ball and cleans the bowl. (Dough will be puffy and soft.)

3 Shape dough into 1-inch balls. Roll balls in egg white and then in nut mixture. Place about 2 inches apart on ungreased baking sheet.

4 Bake *10 to 12 minutes.* Immediately remove from baking sheet. *2 dozen.*

COCONUT-PRUNE MERINGUES

Heavenly little fruit bars in three layers: Short crust, prune and orange filling, coconut meringue.

⅓ cup butter or margarine, softened
¼ cup sugar
1¼ cups Bisquick baking mix
1 tbsp cornstarch
¼ cup sugar
1 cup cut-up pitted cooked prunes
⅓ cup orange juice
1 egg white
2 tbsp sugar
1 cup flaked coconut

Heat oven to 350°

1 Mix butter, ¼ cup sugar and the baking mix. Spread dough evenly in ungreased square pan, 8x8x2 inches.

2 Bake *15 minutes* or until light brown.

3 Blend cornstarch and ¼ cup sugar in saucepan. Stir in prunes and orange juice. Cook, stirring constantly, until mixture thickens and boils. Boil and stir 1 minute. Cool slightly. Spread over baked layer.

4 Beat egg white until foamy. Beat in 2 tablespoons sugar, 1 tablespoon at a time; continue beating until stiff and glossy. Fold in coconut. Spread over prune mixture.

5 Bake *20 to 25 minutes* or until coconut is light brown. Cool thoroughly and cut into bars, 2x1½ inches. *2 dozen.*

PRETTY UP THE COOKIE PLATE With lace paper doilies in white, gold or silver. Hard candies, candied fruit slices or chocolates. A demitasse cup of tiny flowers for the center. Or use an elegant tiered cookie tray.

TUNA IN TULIP CUPS

Lovely for a luncheon. And thrifty, too. If you want to be extra fancy, substitute shrimp or crabmeat.

Cheese Sauce (right)
2 cans (6½ oz each) tuna, drained
2 cups cut-up celery
½ cup chopped salted peanuts
2 tbsp lemon juice
2 tbsp chopped onion
¼ cup mayonnaise or salad dressing
2 cups Bisquick baking mix
½ cup cold water

Heat oven to 425°

1 Prepare Cheese Sauce. Cover to keep warm.

2 Mix tuna, celery, peanuts, lemon juice, onion and mayonnaise; set aside.

3 Stir baking mix and water to a soft dough. Gently smooth dough into a ball on floured cloth-covered board. Knead 5 times.

4 Roll dough into a rectangle, 16x12 inches; cut into twelve 4-inch squares. Place squares in 12 greased medium muffin cups; spoon ⅓ cup tuna mixture into each. Pinch each corner of each square to form 4 points.

5 Bake *15 to 20 minutes.* Serve with warm Cheese Sauce. If you like, garnish each with sliced pimiento-stuffed olives. *6 servings.*

CHEESE SAUCE

¼ cup butter or margarine
¼ cup Bisquick baking mix
½ tsp salt
¼ tsp pepper
2 cups milk
1 cup shredded sharp Cheddar cheese (about 4 oz)

Melt butter over low heat in saucepan. Blend in baking mix and seasonings. Cook over low heat, stirring constantly, until mixture is smooth and bubbly. Remove from heat and stir in milk. Heat to boiling, stirring constantly. Boil and stir 1 minute. Stir in cheese. Heat over low heat, stirring constantly, until cheese is melted.

LADIES' LUNCHEON

Tuna in Tulip Cups with Cheese Sauce
Fresh Fruit Salad
Almond Butterballs (page 57)
Mocha Dessert Coffee (below)

MOCHA DESSERT COFFEE
For each serving, place 1 to 2 tablespoons Betty Crocker canned chocolate frosting in cup. Fill with hot coffee and stir until blended. Go ahead, live it up — garnish with whipped cream.

CRABMEAT SALAD PIE

An elegant do-ahead entree that waits in the refrigerator. Nice with white wine for an after-the-theatre supper.

9-inch Short Pie Shell (page 61)
2 cans (7½ oz each) crabmeat, drained and cartilage removed
2 cups chopped celery
1 cup mayonnaise or salad dressing
2 tbsp lemon juice
2 tsp chopped onion
1 tsp salt
½ cup crushed potato chips

Bake pie shell. Cool. Mix crabmeat, celery, mayonnaise, lemon juice, onion and salt. Pile into pie shell. Cover and chill. Just before serving, sprinkle with potato chips. If you like, *garnish with tomato wedges. 6 to 8 servings.*

CRUSTY CURRIED CHICKEN

Perfect for buffet service with mustard-glazed fruits and one of the breads on page 54.

¼ cup shortening
¼ cup butter or margarine
1 cup Bisquick baking mix
1½ tsp salt
¼ tsp pepper
⅛ tsp curry powder
Two 2½- to 3-lb broiler-fryer chickens, cut up

Heat oven to 425°

1 Melt 2 tablespoons shortening and 2 tablespoons butter in oven in each of 2 oblong pans, 13x9x2 inches.

2 Blend baking mix and seasonings; coat chicken pieces. Place chicken skin side down in shortening mixture.

3 Cook uncovered *40 minutes. Reduce oven temperature to 375°.* Turn chicken and cook *20 minutes longer. 6 to 8 servings.*

BUTTERFLY SHRIMP

Pictured on the chapter cover. For dinner at 8 by candlelight, serve with your own cocktail sauce, buttered asparagus, avocado and grapefruit salad.

1 lb cleaned shrimp
1 cup Bisquick baking mix
2 eggs
½ cup cold water
½ tsp salt

Heat fat or oil (1½ inches) to 375° in electric skillet.

1 Cut slit lengthwise in shrimp but do not cut completely through. Flatten shrimp and pat dry.

2 Stir remaining ingredients until smooth. Dip shrimp into batter.

3 Fry in hot fat ½ to 1 minute on each side or until golden brown. Drain and serve immediately. *4 servings.*

GRASSHOPPER PIE

This pie is designed for applause. The crust is rich and chocolaty, the filling features two famous liqueurs.

9-INCH CHOCOLATE SHORT PIE SHELL

1 cup Bisquick baking mix
¼ cup cocoa
2 tbsp sugar
¼ cup butter or margarine, softened
3 tbsp boiling water

Heat oven to 450°

1 Combine baking mix, cocoa, sugar and butter in small bowl. Add water; stir vigorously until dough forms a ball and cleans the bowl. (Dough will be puffy and soft.)

2 Pat dough with lightly floured hands into 9-inch pie pan, bringing up dough to edge of pan.

3 Bake *8 to 10 minutes*. Cool.

FILLING

1 envelope unflavored gelatin
⅓ cup cold water
1 cup chilled whipping cream
½ can (18-oz size) Betty Crocker vanilla pudding (1 cup)
¼ cup white crème de cacao
¼ cup green crème de menthe
Chocolate curls

Sprinkle gelatin on water in small saucepan to soften. Stir over very low heat until gelatin is dissolved. In chilled bowl, beat cream until stiff. Blend pudding and liqueurs into whipped cream; fold in gelatin and, if you like, green food color. Pour mixture into pie shell. Chill at least 4 hours or until set. Just before serving, garnish with chocolate curls.

Remove chilled pies from refrigerator 20 minutes before serving.

APRICOT MALLOW PIE

*Another beauty queen. Light,
refreshing apricot mallow in a
buttery crust.*

9-INCH SHORT PIE SHELL

1 cup Bisquick baking mix
¼ cup butter or margarine,
   softened
3 tbsp boiling water

Heat oven to 450°

1 Combine baking mix and
   butter in small bowl. Add
   water; stir vigorously until
   dough forms a ball and cleans
   the bowl. (Dough will be puffy
   and soft.)

2 Pat dough with floured hands
   into 9-inch pie pan, bringing
   up dough to edge of pan. If
   you like, flute edge.

3 Bake *8 to 10 minutes.* Cool.

FILLING

32 marshmallows or 3 cups
   miniature marshmallows
¼ cup milk
2 jars (7¾ oz each) chopped
   apricots with tapioca
   (junior food)
1½ cups chilled whipping cream

Combine marshmallows, milk
and apricots in saucepan. Cook
over low heat, stirring
constantly, just until
marshmallows are melted.
Chill until partially set. In
chilled bowl, beat cream until
stiff; fold in marshmallow
mixture. Pile into pie shell.
Chill at least 4 hours or until
set.

CHOCOLATE MOUSSE SHORT PIE

*Chocolate lovers' delight.
Creamy, smooth filling in our
butter-rich pie crust.*

9-inch Short Pie Shell (left)
1 envelope unflavored gelatin
3 tbsp cold water
1 cup chocolate syrup
2 cups chilled whipping cream
½ cup confectioners' sugar
¼ tsp salt

Bake pie shell. Cool. Sprinkle
gelatin on water to soften.
Stir over very low heat until
gelatin is dissolved. Stir into
chocolate syrup. In chilled
bowl, beat cream, sugar and
salt until stiff. Fold into
chocolate mixture. Pile into
pie shell. Chill at least 4 hours
or until set.

BANANA SPLIT STRAWBERRY SHORTCAKE

Here's a teen-time partytime favorite. One gigantic shortcake with banana, strawberries, whipping cream and nuts. Bring it to the table to cut into wedges.

2⅓ cups Bisquick baking mix
3 tbsp sugar
3 tbsp butter or margarine, melted
½ cup milk
2 tbsp soft butter or margarine
1 large banana
1 cup sweetened whipped cream
¼ cup chopped nuts
2 cups sweetened sliced strawberries

Heat oven to 450°

1 Stir baking mix, sugar, 3 tablespoons butter and the milk to a soft dough. Gently smooth dough into a ball on floured cloth-covered board. Knead 8 to 10 times. Divide dough in half.

2 Roll one half into 9-inch circle. Place in ungreased round layer pan, 9x1½ inches; dot with 2 tablespoons butter.

3 Roll other half of dough into 9-inch circle and place on top of dough in pan.

4 Bake *15 minutes* or until light brown. Split warm shortcake crosswise.

5 Slice half the banana over bottom layer and spread with ½ cup of the whipped cream. Sprinkle with 2 tablespoons of the nuts.

6 Place second layer on whipped cream and nuts; slice remaining banana half over top. Spoon strawberries over layers and spread with remaining whipped cream. Sprinkle with remaining nuts. Cut into wedges. *6 to 8 servings.*

STRAWBERRIES SUPREME

A dessert for connoisseurs.

4 cups sliced strawberries
1 cup sugar
2 cups Bisquick baking mix
2 tbsp sugar
¼ cup butter or margarine
2 egg yolks
1 cup dairy sour cream
⅓ cup sugar
Whipped cream

1 Sprinkle strawberries with 1 cup sugar and let stand about 1 hour.

2 Heat oven to 375°. Blend baking mix and 2 tablespoons sugar. Cut in butter until crumbly. Pat mixture in bottom of square pan, 9x9x2 inches.

3 Bake *10 minutes.* Blend egg yolks, sour cream and ⅓ cup sugar; spread over hot baked layer.

4 Bake *20 minutes longer.* Cool thoroughly. Cut into squares and top with sweetened strawberries. Garnish with whipped cream. *9 servings.*

PEACHIE DESSERT WAFFLES

Go gourmet at a do-it-yourself waffle party. Flavor waffles with almond, serve with sour cream-brown sugar topping.

2 cups Bisquick baking mix
2 tbsp salad oil
1 egg
1⅓ cups milk
1 tsp almond extract
½ cup chopped toasted almonds
4 cups sweetened sliced peaches
Sour Cream Topping (below)

1 Beat baking mix, oil, egg, milk and extract with rotary beater until smooth. Stir in almonds.

2 Pour batter from cup or pitcher onto center of hot waffle iron.

3 Bake until steaming stops. Remove waffle carefully. Serve warm topped with peaches and Sour Cream Topping. *Three 9-inch waffles.*

SOUR CREAM TOPPING
Blend 1 cup dairy sour cream and ¼ cup brown sugar (packed).

WAFFLE RASPBERRY SUNDAES

A dessert that makes a meal for guests at Sunday brunch. Serve with lots of hot coffee.

3 eggs, separated
2 cups Bisquick baking mix
1 tbsp sugar
1¼ cups light cream
1 tsp vanilla
4 cups raspberries
1 qt vanilla ice cream

1 Beat egg whites with rotary beater until soft peaks form. Blend baking mix, sugar, light cream, egg yolks and vanilla. Fold egg whites into egg yolk mixture.

2 Pour batter from cup or pitcher onto center of hot waffle iron.

3 Bake until steaming stops. Remove waffle carefully. Serve warm topped with raspberries and ice cream. *Three 9-inch waffles.*

STRAWBERRY PANCAKE DELIGHT

Spring this on pancake fans.

2 eggs
¾ cup milk
2⅓ cups Bisquick baking mix
2 tbsp sugar
¼ cup salad oil
Melted butter or margarine
2 cups sweetened halved
**   strawberries**
Dairy sour cream

1 Beat eggs in small mixer bowl on high speed 5 minutes or until thick and lemon colored. Stir in milk, baking mix, sugar and oil.

2 Pour batter from ¼ -cup measuring cup onto medium-hot ungreased griddle.

3 Bake until puffed and bubbles begin to break. Turn and bake other side until golden brown.

4 Stack 3 pancakes, spreading layers with butter. Top each stack with ½ cup strawberries and a spoonful of sour cream. Serve warm. *4 servings.*

STRAWBERRY SHORTCAKE ROYALE

For those who like their strawberry shortcake on cake. The cake's rum-flavored, spooned with strawberries and custard sauce.

1 can (18 oz) Betty Crocker
**   vanilla pudding**
⅓ cup water
4 cups sliced strawberries
1 cup sugar
1½ cups Bisquick baking mix
½ cup sugar
1 egg
½ cup milk or water
2 tbsp shortening
1 tsp rum flavoring

1 Blend pudding and ⅓ cup water; cover and chill.

2 Sprinkle strawberries with 1 cup sugar and let stand about 1 hour.

3 Heat oven to 350°. Blend remaining ingredients in large mixer bowl on low speed ½ minute, scraping bowl frequently. Beat 4 minutes medium speed.

4 Pour batter into greased and floured square pan, 8x8x2 inches.

5 Bake *30 to 35 minutes* or until wooden pick inserted in center comes out clean. Cool slightly and cut into squares. Split squares; spoon sweetened strawberries between and over top. Pour pudding mixture over all. *9 servings.*

DON'T BRUISE THE BERRIES! Unwrap before storing in the refrigerator. Don't wash till ready to use and you preserve both the beauty and flavor.

LOVE & FRIENDSHIP FOODS

LOVE & FRIENDSHIP

These are the happiness foods that say love and kisses to the family or welcome to your friends. They are the presents you bake for daily meals, snacktime and spontaneous shenanigans. All of the recipes show you how to go homey in a hurry, because that is the nature of Bisquick baking mix.

How's this for starters? Spring a birthday breakfast surprise with Banana Butterscotch Sticky Buns. Invite the neighbors for brunch and make it a do-it-yourself party with Bacon Puff Pancakes. Treat the kaffeeklatsch to speedy Velvet Crumb Cake and serve it warm from the oven. Turn a Sunday night supper into a family party with Corn Dogs and a simple salad served on trays in front of TV. And, for goodness sake, keep that cookie jar filled with after-school treats.

Remember, too, beauty is for everyday. So make the most of pretty plastics, pottery and colorful paper napkins. Turn a budding houseplant into a centerpiece. Switch the table to a view by the window. Vary the ordinary any way and you add a little more love and friendship to everyday.

Betty Crocker

Cranberry-Nut Coffee Cake is pictured on the other side of this page. Recipe on page 71.

APPLE RINGS

Crispy, batter-fried apple rings. Good with any breakfast meat. Or serve with grilled franks for a teenager's kind of breakfast.

1 cup Bisquick baking mix
1 egg
½ cup milk
2 medium apples, pared and
　 cored

1 Beat baking mix, egg and milk with rotary beater until smooth.

2 Slice apples crosswise into ⅛-inch rings. Dip rings into batter.

3 Bake on hot greased griddle until golden brown, turning once. Serve immediately and, if you like, with syrup or jelly or sprinkle with confectioners' sugar. *About 2 dozen.*

DOUGHNUT BALLS

Good morning, Sleepyhead!

¼ cup sugar
½ tsp cinnamon
2 cups Bisquick baking mix
2 tbsp sugar
1 tsp vanilla
1 egg
¼ cup milk
¼ tsp cinnamon
¼ tsp nutmeg

Heat fat or oil (3 to 4 inches) to 375° in deep fat fryer or kettle

1 Mix ¼ cup sugar and ½ teaspoon cinnamon in paper or plastic bag; set aside.

2 Stir baking mix, 2 tablespoons sugar, the vanilla, egg, milk, ¼ teaspoon cinnamon and the nutmeg until smooth.

3 Drop dough by teaspoonfuls into hot fat.

4 Fry about ½ minute on each side or until golden brown. Drain. While warm, shake balls in sugar mixture in bag. *4 dozen.*

THUMBPRINT BISCUITS

Biscuits with jelly in the center. If you're a finicky eater, age 4, what more could you ask of breakfast?

2 cups Bisquick baking mix
½ cup cold water
2 tbsp jelly or jam

Heat oven to 450°

1 Stir baking mix and water to a soft dough.

2 Drop dough by 12 tablespoonfuls onto greased baking sheet. Press floured thumb into center of each mound of dough. Fill each hole with ½ teaspoon jelly. Drop remaining dough by rounded teaspoonfuls onto jelly.

3 Bake *8 to 10 minutes.* Serve warm. *1 dozen.*

BANANA BUTTERSCOTCH STICKY BUNS

*Rich flavor banana buns,
drenched with caramel. Easy
to do. Positively irresistible.*

½ cup brown sugar (packed)
½ cup soft butter or margarine
36 pecan halves
2 cups Bisquick baking mix
⅔ cup mashed ripe banana
2 tbsp soft butter or margarine
¼ cup brown sugar (packed)

Heat oven 450°

1 Place 2 teaspoons brown
sugar, 2 teaspoons butter and
3 pecan halves in each of 12
medium muffin cups. Place in
oven to melt sugar and butter.

2 Stir baking mix and banana to
a soft dough. Gently smooth
dough into a ball on floured
cloth-covered board. Knead
5 times.

3 Roll dough into a rectangle,
15x9 inches. Spread rectangle
with 2 tablespoons butter;
sprinkle with ¼ cup brown
sugar. Roll up tightly,
beginning at wide side. Seal
well by pinching edge of dough
into roll. Cut into twelve
1¼-inch slices. Place slices
cut side down in muffin cups.

4 Bake *10 minutes.* Immediately
invert pan onto baking sheet,
or onto rack with plastic wrap
or waxed paper underneath.
Leave pan over rolls a minute.
Serve warm. *1 dozen.*

SOMEBODY'S BIRTHDAY?
Bake up a surprise for
breakfast. Make it an all-day
celebration and let the birthday
child choose his favorite foods
for every meal. It isn't every
mother who thinks of that
kind of birthday present.

NUT PUFFS

⅓ cup chopped blanched
  almonds
⅓ cup brown sugar (packed)
½ tsp cinnamon
2 cups Bisquick baking mix
⅓ cup raisins
¼ tsp nutmeg
¼ tsp cloves
½ cup cold water
¼ cup butter or margarine,
  melted

Heat oven to 375°

1 Mix almonds, sugar and
  cinnamon; set aside.

2 Stir baking mix, raisins,
  nutmeg, cloves and water to
  a soft dough. Gently smooth
  dough into a ball on floured
  board. Knead 5 times.

3 Shape dough into 12 balls.
  Roll balls in butter and then
  in nut mixture, coating each
  thoroughly. Place in 12
  greased medium muffin cups.

4 Bake *15 to 20 minutes*.
  Serve warm. *1 dozen.*

SPICE-PECAN MUFFINS

2 cups Bisquick baking mix
¼ cup sugar
1 tsp cinnamon
1 tsp allspice
½ cup chopped pecans
1 egg
⅔ cup water or milk
2 tsp sugar

Heat oven to 400°

1 Mix all ingredients except
  2 teaspoons sugar; beat
  vigorously ½ minute.

2 Fill 12 greased medium
  muffin cups ⅔ full. Sprinkle
  with 2 teaspoons sugar.

3 Bake *15 minutes*. Serve warm.
  1 dozen.

BREAKFAST SURPRISES ARE
FUN Quick breads, piping
hot, snuggled in a napkin-
lined basket. Fruit juice in
pretty goblets or punch cups.
A scoop of ice cream in the
cereal bowl. Or fresh fruit
ice-cream sundaes.

ORANGE ROLLS

2⅓ cups Bisquick baking mix
3 tbsp sugar
3 tbsp butter or margarine,
  melted
½ cup milk
2 tbsp soft butter or margarine
½ cup orange marmalade

Heat oven to 425°

1 Stir baking mix, sugar, 3
  tablespoons butter and the
  milk to a soft dough. Gently
  smooth dough into a ball on
  floured cloth-covered board.
  Knead 8 to 10 times.

2 Roll dough into a rectangle,
  15x9 inches. Spread rectangle
  with 2 tablespoons butter and
  the marmalade. Roll up,
  beginning at wide side. Seal
  well by pinching edge of
  dough into roll. Cut into
  1-inch slices.

3 Bake on greased baking sheet
  12 to 15 minutes. Serve warm.
  15 rolls.

CINNAMON BREAD

Tender, flavorful batter bread for the coffee break. Or maybe you prefer tea or hot tomato juice? Then serve butter sandwiches made with Cheese or Herb Bread.

1 pkg active dry yeast
1 cup warm water (105 to 115°)
4 cups Bisquick baking mix
¼ cup sugar
2 tsp cinnamon
Soft butter or margarine

1 Dissolve yeast in warm water in large mixer bowl. Add 2 cups of the baking mix and 2 tablespoons of the sugar. Blend ½ minute on low speed, scraping bowl constantly. Beat 3 minutes medium speed, scraping bowl occasionally. (By hand, beat 400 vigorous strokes.)

2 Stir in remaining baking mix until smooth. Scrape batter from side of bowl. Cover and let rise in warm place until double, about 30 minutes.

3 Stir down batter by beating 25 strokes. Gently fold in remaining sugar and the cinnamon.

4 Spread batter evenly in greased loaf pan, 9x5x3 inches. Smooth top of batter by patting into shape with floured hand. Cover and let rise about 35 minutes.

5 Heat oven to 375°. Bake *35 to 40 minutes* or until well browned. Immediately remove from pan; brush loaf with butter. Cool slightly before cutting. Serve warm. *1 loaf.*

CHEESE BREAD   Omit 2 tablespoons sugar and the cinnamon. Stir in ⅓ cup shredded Cheddar cheese and 2 tablespoons finely chopped pimiento with the second addition of baking mix.

HERB BREAD   Omit 2 tablespoons sugar and the cinnamon. Stir in 2 teaspoons caraway seed, 1 teaspoon crumbled leaf sage and ½ teaspoon nutmeg with the second addition of baking mix.

QUICK RAISIN BREAD

No yeast, no fuss — just mix and roll out on a baking sheet. Bring it to the table on a bread-board and let everyone break off a chunk.

¼ cup sugar
½ tsp cinnamon
2 cups Bisquick baking mix
½ cup cold water
¼ cup raisins
2 tbsp sugar

Heat oven to 450°

1 Mix ¼ cup sugar and the cinnamon; set aside.

2 Stir baking mix, water, raisins and 2 tablespoons sugar to a soft dough.

3 Roll dough on greased baking sheet into a rectangle, 10x8 inches. Spread rectangle with butter and sprinkle with sugar mixture.

4 Bake *10 minutes.* Serve hot. *6 servings.*

BANANA COFFEE CAKE

2 cups Bisquick baking mix
¼ cup sugar
3 tbsp butter or margarine, softened
1 egg
¼ cup milk
¾ cup mashed ripe banana
½ cup chopped nuts
Creamy Icing (below)
¼ cup finely chopped nuts

Heat oven to 400°

1 Combine baking mix, sugar, butter, egg, milk, banana and ½ cup nuts; beat vigorously ½ minute.

2 Spread batter in greased round layer pan, 9x1½ inches.

3 Bake *20 to 25 minutes.* While warm, spread with Creamy Icing and sprinkle with ¼ cup nuts. *8 servings.*

CREAMY ICING Blend ⅓ cup confectioners' sugar and 2 teaspoons milk.

CRANBERRY-NUT COFFEE CAKE

New neighbors to welcome? That calls for a coffee party and something like this from the scrumptious department. See it pictured on the chapter cover.

¼ cup brown sugar (packed)
½ cup chopped walnuts
¼ tsp cinnamon
2 cups Bisquick baking mix
2 tbsp granulated sugar
1 egg
⅔ cup water or milk
⅔ cup whole cranberry sauce
Confectioners' Sugar Icing (right)

Heat oven to 400°

1 Mix brown sugar, walnuts and cinnamon; set aside.

2 Combine baking mix, granulated sugar, egg and water; beat vigorously ½ minute.

3 Spread batter in greased square pan, 9x9x2 inches; sprinkle with nut mixture. Spoon cranberry sauce over top.

4 Bake *20 to 25 minutes.* While warm, spread with Confectioners' Sugar Icing. *9 servings.*

CONFECTIONERS' SUGAR ICING Blend 1 cup confectioners' sugar, ½ teaspoon vanilla and about 1 tablespoon water.

COFFEETIME CUES Just once through for review, the coffee maker's pledge: "A clean pot, fresh cold water from the tap and accurate measurements." Bring out your mod mugs or pottery cups. And how about flowers from the supermarket for the coffee table?

LEMON COFFEE CAKE

Coffee party shower? Why not!

1 tbsp butter or margarine,
  melted
½ cup sugar
1 tbsp grated lemon peel
2 cups Bisquick baking mix
2 tbsp sugar
2 tsp grated lemon peel
1 egg
⅔ cup water or milk

Heat oven to 400°

1 Mix butter, ½ cup sugar and
  1 tablespoon lemon peel;
  set aside.

2 Combine baking mix, 2
  tablespoons sugar, 2 teaspoons
  lemon peel, the egg and water;
  beat vigorously ½ minute.

3 Spread batter in greased
  round layer pan, 9x1½ inches.
  Sprinkle sugar mixture over
  batter.

4 Bake *20 to 25 minutes. Serve
  warm. 8 servings.*

ORANGE-NUTMEG COFFEE CAKE

Try it with iced coffee.

2 cups Bisquick baking mix
2 tbsp sugar
2 tbsp grated orange peel
1 egg
2 tbsp salad oil
⅔ cup water or milk
Nutmeg Topping (below)

Heat oven to 400°

1 Combine baking mix, sugar,
  orange peel, egg, oil and
  water; beat vigorously
  ½ minute.

2 Spread batter in greased
  round layer pan, 9x1½ inches.
  Sprinkle Nutmeg Topping
  over batter.

3 Bake *20 to 25 minutes. Serve
  warm. 8 servings.*

NUTMEG TOPPING   Mix ¼
cup sugar, 2 tablespoons
Bisquick baking mix, 2
tablespoons firm butter or
margarine and ½ teaspoon
nutmeg until crumbly.

PEANUT BUTTER & JELLY COFFEE CAKE

*Kids aren't the only ones who
love this combination of
flavors. Try it on the girls'
bowling team or the men's
poker club.*

2 cups Bisquick baking mix
2 tbsp sugar
¼ cup creamy peanut butter
1 egg
⅔ cup water or milk
½ cup jelly or jam

Heat oven to 400°

1 Stir together baking mix and
  sugar; cut in peanut butter.
  Add milk and egg; beat
  vigorously ½ minute.

2 Spread batter in greased
  round layer pan, 9x1½ inches.
  Spoon jelly over batter,
  spreading thinly.

3 Bake *25 to 30 minutes. Serve
  warm. 8 servings.*

VELVET CRUMB CAKE

*Want to do something nice for
an afternoon coffee party?
Try this, warm from the oven.
And have an extra pot of coffee
perking in the kitchen.*

1½ cups Bisquick baking mix
½ cup sugar
1 egg
½ cup milk or water
2 tbsp shortening
1 tsp vanilla
Honey Crisp Topping (right)

Heat oven to 350°

1 Blend all ingredients except
topping in large mixer bowl
on low speed ½ minute,
scraping bowl frequently.
Beat 4 minutes medium speed.

2 Pour batter into greased and
floured square pan, 8x8x2
inches, or round layer pan,
9x1½ inches.

3 Bake *30 to 35 minutes* or until
wooden pick inserted in center
comes out clean. While warm,
spread with Honey Crisp
Topping.

4 Set oven control at broil
and/or 550°. Place cake about
3 inches from heat; broil about
3 minutes or until mixture is
nicely browned.

HONEY CRISP TOPPING   Mix
3 tablespoons butter or
margarine, softened, ⅓ cup
honey, ¼ cup shredded
coconut, ½ cup crushed
Wheaties® cereal and 1 can
(8½ ounces) crushed
pineapple, drained.

COCONUT BROILED TOPPING
Mix ½ cup flaked coconut,
⅓ cup brown sugar (packed),
¼ cup chopped nuts,
3 tablespoons soft butter or
margarine and 2 tablespoons
light cream.

PANCAKES

Bake them plain or try one of the variations. Then go fancy with the syrups (page 75). Or spread with whipped butter and sprinkle with confectioners' sugar.

2 cups Bisquick baking mix
1 egg
1⅓ cups milk

1 Beat all ingredients with rotary beater until smooth.

2 Pour batter from ¼-cup measuring cup onto heated griddle. (Grease griddle if necessary.)

3 Bake until bubbles appear. Turn and bake other side until golden brown. *About 18.*

APPLE PANCAKES Fold 2 cups finely chopped unpared apple (about 2 medium), 2 tablespoons sugar and 1 tablespoon lemon juice into batter.

BACON PANCAKES Fold 4 slices bacon, crisply fried and crumbled, into batter.

BANANA PANCAKES Fold 1 cup mashed ripe bananas (about 2 medium) and 2 tablespoons sugar into batter.

COCONUT PANCAKES Fold 1 cup shredded coconut into batter.

ORANGE-NUT PANCAKES Fold 2 tablespoons grated orange peel and ⅓ cup finely chopped pecans into batter.

NOTE Keep pancakes hot between layers of paper towels in a low oven.

HOW ABOUT A PANCAKE PAJAMA PARTY? For the family only, on a leisurely Sunday morning. Guests come as they are, in their bathrobes, and sip Sparkling Orange Juice while they read the Sunday comics. (Two parts orange juice to one part chilled carbonated lemon beverage, with a slice of orange afloat.) Everybody takes his turn at the griddle — flips his own pancakes, rolls them up with lots of brown sugar or jam — helps himself to the pork sausages staying warm in the oven. No alarm clocks, no rules, nobody's counting. It's a family holiday.

PUFF PANCAKES

Tender, light pancakes with a delicate lacy crust. Extra special for planned or instant hospitality.

2 eggs
¾ cup milk
2⅓ cups Bisquick baking mix
2 tbsp sugar
¼ cup salad oil

1 Beat eggs in small mixer bowl on high speed 5 minutes or until thick and lemon colored. Stir in remaining ingredients.

2 Pour batter from ¼-cup measuring cup onto medium-hot ungreased griddle.

3 Bake until puffed and bubbles begin to break. Turn and bake other side until golden brown. *About 12.*

BACON PUFF PANCAKES
Fold 8 slices bacon, crisply fried and crumbled, into batter.

BLUEBERRY PUFF PANCAKES
Fold 1 cup well-drained blueberries into batter.

CORN PUFF PANCAKES
Fold 1 cup drained whole kernel corn into batter.

HAM PUFF PANCAKES
Fold 1½ cups finely chopped cooked ham into batter.

PECAN PUFF PANCAKES
Fold 1 cup finely chopped pecans into batter.

SPICY PUFF PANCAKES
Fold 1 teaspoon cinnamon and ½ teaspoon *each* allspice, cloves and nutmeg into batter.

BRUNCH-LUNCH MEATS IN MINUTES Place separated bacon slices or pork sausages on rack in pan. Bake in 400° oven. Bacon takes 10 minutes, no turning. Pork sausages take 20 to 30 minutes, turning once.

SYRUPS

Serve hot syrup in a coffee carafe over a candle warmer.

CINNAMON-MAPLE SYRUP
Heat 1 cup maple-flavored syrup, 1 tablespoon butter or margarine and ½ teaspoon cinnamon, stirring occasionally. *1 cup.*

MAPLE-APRICOT SYRUP
Heat ¾ cup maple-flavored syrup, 1 tablespoon butter or margarine and ¼ cup apricot nectar, stirring occasionally. *1 cup.*

MAPLE-NUT SYRUP
Heat 1 cup maple-flavored syrup and 1 tablespoon butter or margarine. Remove from heat and stir in ¼ cup chopped pecans or toasted almonds. *About 1 cup.*

ORANGE-MAPLE SYRUP
Heat 1 cup maple-flavored syrup, grated peel of 1 orange and 1 tablespoon butter or margarine, stirring occasionally. *1 cup.*

WAFFLES

Plain waffles, nut waffles, waffles with fruit — they're all grand. Especially with Sausage Ball Syrup. And don't forget about waffles with chicken à la king.

2 cups Bisquick baking mix
2 tbsp salad oil
1 egg
1⅓ cups milk

1 Beat all ingredients with rotary beater until smooth.

2 Pour batter from cup or pitcher onto center of hot waffle iron.

3 Bake until steaming stops. Remove waffle carefully. *Three 9-inch waffles.*

BACON WAFFLES Place short slices of lightly browned bacon on grids; pour batter over bacon.

BANANA WAFFLES Fold 2 tablespoons sugar and ½ cup mashed ripe banana (1 medium) into batter.

BLUEBERRY WAFFLES Fold 2 tablespoons sugar and 1 cup well-drained blueberries into batter.

NUT WAFFLES Fold ¾ cup finely chopped pecans, peanuts or walnuts into batter.

SPICY WAFFLES Fold 1 teaspoon cinnamon, ½ teaspoon *each* allspice, cloves and nutmeg into batter.

SAUSAGE BALL SYRUP
Shape ½ pound bulk pork sausage into 1-inch balls. Cook over medium heat about 10 minutes, turning frequently. Drain. In saucepan, heat sausage balls and 1⅓ cups maple-flavored syrup to boiling. Serve hot.

NUT BREAD

Moist, tender bread that adds a change of pace to any brunch or lunch. See the index for a variety of flavors.

3 cups Bisquick baking mix
½ cup sugar
⅓ cup Gold Medal flour*
1 egg
1 cup milk
1½ cups chopped nuts

Heat oven to 350°

1 Combine baking mix, sugar, flour, egg and milk; beat vigorously ½ minute. Stir in nuts.

2 Pour batter into greased loaf pan, 9x5x3 inches.

3 Bake *55 to 60 minutes* or until wooden pick inserted in center comes out clean. Cool thoroughly before slicing.

*Do not use self-rising flour in this recipe.

LUNCHBOX SANDWICHES
For lunches that travel to school or the office, introduce something different with nut bread sandwiches. Fill with softened butter, peanut butter and jelly, cream cheese, orange marmalade, apple or honey butter.

SALAD DAY LUNCHES   Your
turn for bridge? Serve a fresh fruit plate or chicken salad with open-face nut bread sandwiches. Slice nut bread, cut into fancy shapes and spread with Orange Butter: Mix ½ cup soft butter or margarine, 1 tablespoon orange juice and 1 teaspoon grated orange peel.

SOLO LUNCHES   At home
alone for lunch? Enjoy a slice of nut bread plain with cottage cheese and fruit, a cup of hot tea or bouillon.

DATE NUT BREAD

3 cups Bisquick baking mix
⅓ cup sugar
⅓ cup Gold Medal flour
2 eggs
1 cup milk
1½ cups cut-up dates
¾ cup finely chopped almonds
1 tsp grated lemon peel
Lemon Butter (below)

Heat oven to 350°

1 Combine baking mix, sugar, flour, eggs and milk; beat vigorously ½ minute. Stir in dates, nuts and lemon peel.

2 Pour batter into greased loaf pan, 9x5x3 inches.

3 Bake *about 1 hour* or until wooden pick inserted in center comes out clean. Cool thoroughly before slicing. Spread slices with Lemon Butter.

LEMON BUTTER   Blend ¼
cup butter or margarine, softened, and ¼ teaspoon grated lemon peel.

MUFFINS

De-licious with a bowl of hot soup for lunch. Or alongside hot chili or scrambled eggs. Or, you name it — and choose your favorite muffin flavor.

2 cups Bisquick baking mix
2 tbsp sugar
1 egg
⅔ cup water or milk

Heat oven to 400°

1 Mix all ingredients; beat vigorously ½ minute.

2 Fill 12 greased medium muffin cups ⅔ full.

3 Bake *15 minutes.* Serve warm. *1 dozen.*

BACON MUFFINS Fold ¼ cup crumbled crisply fried bacon (about 6 slices) into batter.

BLUEBERRY MUFFINS Fold 1 cup fresh or ¾ cup well-drained canned blueberries into batter.

BRAN MUFFINS Fold 1 cup bran into batter.

OATMEAL MUFFINS Fold ¾ cup oats into batter.

ORANGE MUFFINS Measure juice from 1 orange and enough water to measure ½ cup liquid; omit water or milk.

BRING LEFTOVERS BACK WITH STYLE Split, butter and toast under the broiler. Or wrap leftover muffins in foil and place in preheated 400° oven 5 to 10 minutes. You'll still say de-licious.

BAKED ITALIAN BURGERS

Spicy beef burgers baked in the oven with cheese-topped biscuits. Hold the thought for spur-of-the-moment family suppers or drop-in company.

1 lb ground beef
1 egg
¼ cup chopped green pepper
1 clove garlic, minced
1 tsp salt
1 tsp oregano
½ tsp Worcestershire sauce
Dash of pepper
½ cup Bisquick baking mix
⅓ cup tomato sauce
2 cups Bisquick baking mix
½ cup cold water
⅓ cup shredded mozzarella or
   Romano cheese

Heat oven to 400°

1 Mix all ingredients except 2 cups baking mix, the water and cheese; shape mixture into 6 patties. Place patties on rack in shallow pan.

2 Stir 2 cups baking mix and the water to a soft dough. Gently smooth dough into a ball on floured cloth-covered board. Knead 5 times.

3 Roll dough ½ inch thick. Cut with floured 2½-inch cutter. Place biscuits on rack with patties.

4 Bake *20 minutes.* Sprinkle patties with cheese.
   To serve, split biscuits and place patties between halves. *6 servings.*

STAY FOR SUPPER
Baked Italian Burgers
Italian Salad   Ripe Olives
Fresh Fruit
Chianti

BROILER SANDWICHES

Tomato, ham and cheese on top.

2 cups Bisquick baking mix
½ cup cold water
2 tbsp soft butter or margarine
8 thin slices tomato (1 large)
8 slices cooked ham
Prepared mustard
8 slices process American
   cheese

Heat oven to 450°

1 Stir baking mix and water to a soft dough.

2 Roll dough into a rectangle, 12x8 inches, on greased baking sheet; spread rectangle with butter.

3 Bake *10 minutes.* Cut into 8 rectangles.

4 Top each with tomato and ham slice; spread ham with mustard. Place cheese slice on ham slice.

5 Set oven control at broil and/or 550°. Broil 6 inches from heat about 3 minutes or until cheese is bubbly. Serve immediately. *8 sandwiches.*

CHEESEBURGER IN A BUN

You'll rival the local drive-in with this one. Broiled hamburger, with tomato and cheese slices, baked in a giant-size bun. Groovy, Mom, with deli dills and lots of catsup.

1½ lb ground beef
3 slices bacon, diced
¼ cup chopped onion
1 tsp salt
⅛ tsp pepper
2⅓ cups Bisquick baking mix
3 tbsp butter or margarine, melted
½ cup milk
6 slices tomato
6 slices process American cheese

Set oven control at broil and/or 550°

1 Mix ground beef, bacon, onion, salt and pepper; shape mixture into 6 patties. Place patties on rack in broiler pan.

2 Broil 3 to 4 inches from heat 4 to 5 minutes on each side.

3 Decrease oven temperature to 400°. Stir baking mix, butter and milk to a soft dough. Gently smooth dough into a ball on floured cloth-covered board. Knead 8 to 10 times.

4 Roll dough ⅛ inch thick. Cut with floured 4½-inch cutter.

5 Place half of the rounds of dough on ungreased baking sheet. Place 1 meat patty, 1 slice tomato and 1 slice cheese on each round. Top with remaining rounds. Pinch edges together to seal securely; cut slit in center of each.

6 Bake *15 minutes* or until golden brown. *6 servings.*

CHICKEN 'N DUMPLINGS

A quick and easy way to use up Sunday's chicken. Good idea for brides and working wives.

2 to 3 cups cut-up cooked
   chicken or turkey
1 can (16 oz) whole onions
1 can (16 oz) sliced carrots
1 can (16 oz) cut-up green beans
1¼ cups chicken broth*
1½ tsp barbecue spice
½ tsp salt
¼ tsp thyme
2 cups Bisquick baking mix
¼ tsp dill weed
⅔ cup milk

1 Combine chicken, onions (with liquid), carrots (with liquid), green beans (with liquid), chicken broth, barbecue spice, salt and thyme. Heat to boiling, stirring occasionally.

2 Stir remaining ingredients to a soft dough. Drop dough by spoonfuls onto boiling chicken mixture.

3 Cook uncovered over low heat 10 minutes; cover and cook 10 minutes longer. Serve in soup bowls. *6 servings.*

*Use canned chicken broth, or make chicken broth by dissolving 2 chicken bouillon cubes in 1¼ cups boiling water.

CORN DOGS

Franks fried in cornmeal batter — just like carnival time. Think about them for Sunday supper or teentime.

1 cup Bisquick baking mix
2 tbsp yellow cornmeal
½ tsp dry mustard
¼ tsp paprika
⅛ tsp cayenne pepper
1 egg
⅓ cup milk
1 lb frankfurters

Heat fat or oil (1 to 2 inches) to 375° in electric skillet

1 Stir all ingredients except frankfurters until smooth.

2 Dip frankfurters (dry) into batter with tongs, allowing excess batter to drip into bowl. (If batter thickens, thin with small amount of milk.)

3 Fry in hot fat 3 minutes on each side or until brown. Drain. *4 or 5 servings.*

MEATBALL VEGETABLE CASSEROLE

Here's what we call everyday excitement. Meatballs and vegetables are flavored with sour cream, golden biscuits bake on top and it all goes together in a hurry.

1 lb ground beef
3 tbsp dairy sour cream
¼ cup chopped onion
1 tbsp snipped parsley
1 tsp salt
⅛ tsp pepper
1 can (10½ oz) condensed
   cream of celery soup
3 tbsp dairy sour cream
1 can (16 oz) peas, green
   beans or sliced carrots
1 can (15 oz) potatoes,
   drained and sliced
2 cups Bisquick baking mix
½ cup cold water

Heat oven to 450°

1 Mix ground beef, 3 tablespoons sour cream, the onion, parsley, salt and pepper. Shape mixture into 1-inch balls; place in ungreased baking dish, 11½x7½x1½ inches.

2 Bake *8 to 12 minutes* or until meatballs are brown.

3 Mix soup, 3 tablespoons sour cream, the peas (with liquid) and potatoes; pour over meatballs. Keep hot in oven while preparing biscuits.

4 Stir baking mix and water to a soft dough. Gently smooth dough into a ball on floured cloth-covered board. Knead 5 times.

5 Roll dough ½ inch thick. Cut with floured 2-inch cutter. Place on hot vegetable mixture.

6 Bake *15 to 20 minutes* or until biscuits are golden brown. *4 to 6 servings.*

FAMILY SUPPER SPECIAL
Tomato Juice with Crisp
   Relishes
Meatball Vegetable Casserole
Salad Greens
Spice Cupcakes (page 83)
Coffee   Milk

SALMON RAREBIT PIE

Double quick meal-in-a-casserole. For after a day of shopping, politicking or committee meetings.

1 can (16 oz) salmon, drained
1 can (8 oz) peas, drained
1 can (10½ oz) condensed
   Cheddar cheese soup
2 tbsp milk
2 cups Bisquick baking mix
½ cup cold water

Heat oven to 450°

1 Mix salmon, peas, soup and milk in ungreased square pan, 8x8x2 inches. Heat in oven 10 minutes.

2 Stir baking mix and water to a soft dough. Gently smooth dough into a ball on floured cloth-covered board. Knead 5 times.

3 Roll dough ½ inch thick. Cut with floured 2-inch cutter. Place biscuits on hot salmon mixture.

4 Bake *15 minutes* or until biscuits are golden brown. *4 to 6 servings.*

APPLE CRUNCH

The flavors of caramel apples, served warm, along with biscuit topping. A cozy kind of dessert to curl up with in front of TV.

Caramel Sauce (right)
5 cups sliced pared apples
　(about 5 medium)
½ tsp cinnamon
¼ tsp nutmeg
1½ cups Bisquick baking mix
½ cup milk
⅛ tsp cinnamon

1 Prepare Caramel Sauce. Cool.

2 Heat oven to 400°. Place apples in ungreased square pan, 8x8x2 inches. Sprinkle with ½ teaspoon cinnamon and the nutmeg.

3 Stir baking mix and milk to a soft dough. Spread dough over apples; sprinkle with ⅛ teaspoon cinnamon. Pour Caramel Sauce over top.

4 Bake *35 minutes* or until apples are tender. *6 servings.*

CARAMEL SAUCE

¼ cup Bisquick baking mix
1 cup brown sugar (packed)
½ tsp salt
1 tsp vinegar
1 cup water
1 tsp vanilla
1 tbsp butter or margarine

Blend baking mix, sugar and salt in saucepan. Stir in vinegar and water. Cook, stirring constantly, over medium heat until mixture thickens and boils. Boil and stir 1 minute. Remove from heat. Stir in vanilla and butter.

SPICE CUPCAKES

Our prized Velvet Crumb Cake goes spicy for cupcakes. They're moist and nice for the lunchbox, just right for afternoon tea.

1½ cups Bisquick baking mix
½ cup sugar
1½ tsp pumpkin pie spice
1 egg
½ cup milk or water
2 tbsp shortening
1 tsp vanilla

Heat oven to 375°

1 Blend all ingredients in large mixer bowl on low speed ½ minute, scraping bowl frequently. Beat 4 minutes medium speed.

2 Fill 16 greased medium muffin cups or paper-lined muffin cups about ⅓ full.

3 Bake *about 15 minutes* or until wooden pick inserted in center comes out clean. Cool. If you like, frost with Browned Butter Frosting (page 86). *16 cupcakes.*

CHOCOLATE-CINNAMON DESSERT

Chocolate-cinnamon cake à la mode with the flavors repeated in the sauce. Serve warm on a wintry night, cold on a summer's evening.

1⅓ cups Bisquick baking mix
½ cup sugar
⅓ cup cocoa
1 tsp cinnamon
1 egg
⅔ cup milk
3 tbsp butter or margarine, softened
1 pt vanilla ice cream
Chocolate-Cinnamon Sauce (right)

Heat oven to 350°

1 Blend all ingredients except ice cream and sauce in large mixer bowl on low speed ½ minute, scraping bowl frequently. Beat 4 minutes medium speed.

2 Pour batter into greased and floured square pan, 8x8x2 inches.

3 Bake *35 to 40 minutes* or until wooden pick inserted in center comes out clean. Serve warm or cool with ice cream and Chocolate-Cinnamon Sauce.

CHOCOLATE-CINNAMON SAUCE Mix 1 cup chocolate syrup and 1 teaspoon cinnamon.

ANYTIME SNACKS Set out fresh fruits and vegetables. For a tasty dip, try Dill Dunk: Blend ⅔ cup mayonnaise, ⅔ cup dairy sour cream, 1 tablespoon parsley flakes, 1 teaspoon dill weed, 1 teaspoon seasoned salt — and, if appetites are willing, a dash of garlic salt.

BEDTIME SNACKS Fresh fruits and cereals make light and refreshing bites-to-eat. Or solo the cereals and top with chocolate milk for a change, softened ice cream or sherbet.

QUICK PEACH COBBLER

A home-sweet-homey dessert.

1 can (29 oz) sliced peaches
3 tbsp cornstarch
½ tsp cinnamon
1 cup Bisquick baking mix
1 tbsp sugar
¼ cup milk
¼ cup dairy sour cream

Heat oven to 400°

1 Combine peaches (with syrup), cornstarch and cinnamon in large saucepan. Cook, stirring constantly, until mixture thickens and boils. Boil and stir 1 minute. Pour into ungreased 1½-quart casserole. Keep hot in oven while preparing topping.

2 Stir remaining ingredients to a soft dough.

3 Drop dough by 6 spoonfuls onto hot peach mixture.

4 Bake *20 to 25 minutes* or until topping is light brown. Serve warm. *6 servings.*

CANDY BAR BROWNIES

Chewy, golden brownies with bits of chocolate and nuts. Doubly good when shared as an after-school snack with a friend.

¾ cup brown sugar (packed)
1 egg
1 tbsp water
1⅓ cups Bisquick baking mix
½ cup chopped chocolate-covered peanuts

Heat oven to 375°

1 Mix sugar, egg and water; stir in baking mix and candy.
2 Spread dough in greased square pan, 8x8x2 inches.
3 Bake *30 to 35 minutes*. While warm, cut into squares. *About 16.*

NOTE If you like, sprinkle brownies with confectioners' sugar. And remember brownies and milk are perfect partners at snacktime.

GOLDEN GOODIE BARS

So rich, they're almost like candy bars. Use them for lunchbox treats and you can hold eager eaters to a quota.

2 cups Bisquick baking mix
1½ cups brown sugar (packed)
3 eggs
1 tsp vanilla
1 cup chopped nuts
½ cup flaked coconut

Heat oven to 350°

1 Blend baking mix, sugar, eggs and vanilla in large bowl; stir in nuts and coconut.
2 Spread dough in greased and floured oblong pan, 13x9x2 inches.
3 Bake *about 35 minutes*. Cool and cut into bars, 2x1 inch. *4½ dozen.*

BROWN SUGAR DROPS

½ cup butter or margarine,
  softened
1¼ cups brown sugar (packed)
2 eggs
1 tsp vanilla
3½ cups Bisquick baking mix

Heat oven to 375°

1 Mix all ingredients.

2 Drop dough by teaspoonfuls onto ungreased baking sheet.

3 Bake *10 to 12 minutes* or until light brown. Cool. If you like, frost with Browned Butter Frosting (below). *About 4 dozen.*

BROWNED BUTTER
FROSTING Heat ⅓ cup butter or margarine in saucepan over medium heat until a delicate brown. Blend in 3 cups confectioners' sugar. Stir in 1½ teaspoons vanilla and about 2 tablespoons milk; beat until frosting is smooth and of spreading consistency.

PEANUT BUTTER COOKIES

A quick way to make tender, tasty peanut butter cookies. For munching, picnicking or treating the neighborhood kids.

1 cup peanut butter
¼ cup shortening
½ cup granulated sugar
½ cup brown sugar (packed)
⅓ cup water
2 cups Bisquick baking mix

Heat oven to 400°

1 Mix peanut butter, shortening, sugars and water; stir in baking mix.

2 Shape dough by scant teaspoonfuls into balls. Place on ungreased baking sheet. With fork dipped in flour, flatten in crisscross pattern.

3 Bake *5 to 7 minutes. About 4½ dozen.*

PUDDING COOKIES

Cookies in ten minutes. And you name the flavor with your choice of instant pudding.

1 cup Bisquick baking mix
1 pkg (about 3½ or 4½ oz)
  instant pudding
¼ cup salad oil
1 egg

Heat oven to 350°

1 Mix all ingredients until dough forms a ball.

2 Shape dough by teaspoonfuls into balls. Place on ungreased baking sheet. Dip bottom of glass into sugar; flatten balls.

3 Bake *about 8 minutes. 2½ to 3 dozen.*

AMERICAN FAVORITES

AMERICAN FAVORITES

Sharing recipes is fun; sharing a little local color makes it even more fun — which is one way recipe swapping took hold in this country, back in covered wagon days. Within this chapter are many of the old recipes that passed from friend to friend, generation after generation, and eventually became all-time, all-American favorites.

Some of these recipes conjure up memories of colonial days — like Bay State Cranberry Pudding and Praline Biscuits. Others take your taste traveling to the Midwest for corn in your fritters and Cheddar cheese sauce on tomato shortcakes. Still others let your appetite strike out for all points west; there you can rediscover Tucson Date Cookies, California Coffee Ring and Alaska Salmon Supper.

For the most part, these were once old-fashioned scratch recipes. But take heart, old-fashioned goodness is no trick today. We recapture it with streamlined recipes and Bisquick baking mix. Now aren't you glad you belong to the free and easy era of convenience foods?

Betty Crocker

Scarlett O'Hara Strawberry Shortcake is pictured on preceding page. The recipe is on page 94.

BOSTON CLAM CHOWDER

Different from Manhattan Clam Chowder, this one calls for milk instead of tomatoes. Serve with Plantation Corn Sticks, page 93.

1 pkg Betty Crocker scalloped
  potatoes
1 can (7 to 8 oz) minced clams
  (reserve liquor)
2½ cups milk
1 tbsp butter or margarine

Mix potato slices, Seasoned Sauce Mix, amounts of water and milk called for on package and clam liquor in large saucepan. Heat to boiling, stirring occasionally. Reduce heat; cover and simmer about 25 minutes or until potatoes are tender, stirring occasionally. Stir in clams, 2½ cups milk and the butter; heat through. *6 servings.*

LOBSTER NEWBURG

Reminiscent of the rocky coasts of Maine where lobster is king.

¼ cup butter or margarine
¼ cup Bisquick baking mix
½ tsp salt
¼ tsp pepper
2 cups milk
2 cans (5 oz each) lobster,
  drained and broken into
  pieces
Toast points

1 Melt butter over low heat in saucepan. Blend in baking mix and seasonings.

2 Cook over low heat, stirring until mixture is smooth and bubbly. Remove from heat and stir in milk. Heat to boiling, stirring constantly. Boil and stir 1 minute.

3 Stir in lobster; cook over low heat until heated through. Serve on toast points. *4 servings.*

OLD GREENWICH PUMPKIN MUFFINS

Spiced with nutmeg, of course, since Connecticut is the nutmeg state. Plus a touch of cinnamon and ginger.

2 cups Bisquick baking mix
¼ cup sugar
½ tsp nutmeg
½ tsp cinnamon
½ tsp ginger
1 egg
½ cup canned pumpkin
½ cup milk

Heat oven to 400°

1 Mix all ingredients; beat vigorously ½ minute.

2 Fill 12 greased medium muffin cups or paper-lined muffin cups ⅔ full.

3 Bake *15 minutes* or until golden brown. *1 dozen.*

BAR HARBOR BLUEBERRY COBBLER

1 can (21 oz) blueberry pie
　filling
1 tsp grated orange peel
1 cup Bisquick baking mix
1 tbsp sugar
¼ cup orange juice
1 tbsp butter or margarine,
　softened

Heat oven to 400°

1 Mix pie filling and orange peel in ungreased 1½-quart casserole. Heat in oven 15 minutes while preparing topping.

2 Stir remaining ingredients to a soft dough.

3 Drop dough by 6 spoonfuls onto hot blueberry mixture.

4 Bake *20 to 25 minutes* or until topping is light brown. Serve warm and, if you like, with light cream. *6 servings.*

BAY STATE CRANBERRY PUDDING

2 cups Bisquick baking mix
½ cup sugar
2 tbsp shortening, melted
⅓ cup milk
1 egg
2 cups cranberries
Butter Sauce (below)

Heat oven to 350°

1 Combine baking mix, sugar, shortening, milk and egg; beat vigorously ½ minute. Fold in cranberries.

2 Spread batter in greased and floured square pan, 9x9x2 inches.

3 Bake *about 45 minutes*. While warm, cut into squares and serve with hot Butter Sauce. *9 to 12 servings.*

BUTTER SAUCE　Cook ½ cup butter or margarine, 1 cup sugar and ¾ cup light cream over low heat, stirring constantly, until smooth.

CAPE COD APPLESAUCE CAKE

A new twist for the applesauce cake of old Massachusetts. And this one is iced with spicy cinnamon candy frosting.

1½ cups Bisquick baking mix
½ cup brown sugar (packed)
1 egg
2 tbsp water
½ cup applesauce
2 tbsp shortening
1 tsp vanilla
½ tsp cinnamon
Cinnamon Candy Frosting
   (right)

Heat oven to 350°

1 Blend all ingredients except frosting in large mixer bowl on low speed ½ minute, scraping bowl frequently. Beat 4 minutes medium speed.

2 Pour batter into greased and floured square pan, 8x8x2 inches, or round layer pan, 9x1½ inches.

3 Bake *30 to 35 minutes* or until wooden pick inserted in center comes out clean. Cool. Frost with Cinnamon Candy Frosting. Refrigerate.

CINNAMON CANDY FROSTING
3 tbsp red cinnamon candies
1 tbsp light corn syrup
1 tbsp water
1 egg white

Heat candies, syrup and water in small saucepan over medium heat just to boiling, stirring constantly. Remove from heat. (Candies will not be completely dissolved.) In small mixer bowl, beat egg white on high speed until stiff. Continue beating, pouring hot syrup very slowly in a thin stream into beaten egg white. Beat on high speed until soft peaks form.

VERMONT PANCAKES

Rich, thick, golden pancakes. Turn them into a Vermont dessert with scoops of maple nut ice cream and lots of maple syrup.

2 cups Bisquick baking mix
1 tbsp salad oil
2 eggs
1 cup milk

1 Beat all ingredients with rotary beater until smooth.

2 Pour batter from ¼-cup measuring cup onto heated griddle. (Grease griddle if necessary.)

3 Bake until bubbles appear. Turn and bake other side until golden brown. *About 12.*

COUNTRY-FRIED STEAK

A rich, brown, well-seasoned steak served Southern style with pan gravy. And the gravy's never tricky with Bisquick baking mix.

½ cup Bisquick baking mix
½ tsp salt
⅛ tsp pepper
⅛ tsp paprika
1 lb beef round steak, cut
   into serving-size pieces
2 tbsp shortening
1½ cups water

1 Blend baking mix, salt, pepper and paprika; coat meat pieces. (Reserve remaining seasoned mixture.)

2 Cook meat in hot shortening until brown. Add ¼ cup of the water; cover.

3 Cook over low heat about 2 hours or until meat is tender. Remove meat to platter.

4 Add 1 cup of the water to drippings in skillet. Stir together 2 tablespoons of the reserved seasoned mixture and remaining ¼ cup water. Gradually stir into drippings. Heat to boiling, stirring constantly; boil and stir 1 minute. Pour over meat. *4 servings.*

SOUTHERN HOSPITALITY
Country-fried Steak
Fried Tomatoes
Ambrosia Salad
Plantation Corn Sticks
   (page 93)
Mint Julep Parfaits
Chickory Coffee

DELTA BISCUIT CROWN

⅓ cup butter or margarine
½ to 1 tsp garlic salt or
   onion salt
2 cups Bisquick baking mix
2 tsp caraway seed
½ cup cold water

Heat oven to 450°

1 Melt butter in oven in 6-cup ring mold; sprinkle with garlic salt.

2 Stir remaining ingredients to a soft dough. Gently smooth dough into a ball on floured cloth-covered board. Knead 5 times.

3 Roll dough ½ inch thick. Cut with floured 2-inch cutter. Place biscuits with edges touching in mold.

4 Bake *about 10 minutes.* Invert onto plate and serve warm. *6 to 8 servings.*

FLORIDA HUSH PUPPIES

So the story goes, hunters used to feed corn patties to their dogs to keep them quiet — thus the name Hush Puppies. We suggest you eat these tasty cornmeal morsels yourself with fried fish or chicken.

1 cup Bisquick baking mix
1 cup cornmeal
1 tsp salt
1 egg
¾ cup milk

Heat fat or oil (1 inch deep) to 375° in electric skillet

1 Mix all ingredients thoroughly.

2 Drop batter by teaspoonfuls into hot fat.

3 Fry in hot fat about 2 minutes on each side or until brown. Drain and serve immediately. *15 to 20.*

PLANTATION CORN STICKS

A new way to make them old-fashioned good — fast!

2 eggs
1 cup Bisquick baking mix
1 cup cornmeal
1½ cups buttermilk
2 tbsp salad oil

Heat oven to 450°

1 Heat 12 generously greased corn stick pans, medium muffin cups or square pan, 9x9x2 inches, in oven.

2 Beat eggs with rotary beater until fluffy. Beat in remaining ingredients *just* until smooth.

3 Pour or spoon batter into hot pans.

4 Bake corn sticks and muffins *15 to 20 minutes,* corn bread *20 to 25 minutes.* Serve piping hot and, if you like, with butter. *12 servings.*

PRALINE BISCUITS

Pecans, brown sugar, butter. All Southern-style sweet roll flavors that make you glad you own an appetite.

½ cup butter or margarine, melted
½ cup brown sugar (packed)
24 or 36 pecan halves
Cinnamon
2 cups Bisquick baking mix
½ cup cold water

Heat oven to 425°

1 Place 2 teaspoons butter, 2 teaspoons sugar and 2 or 3 pecan halves in each of 12 greased medium muffin cups. Sprinkle cinnamon in each cup.

2 Stir baking mix and water to a soft dough.

3 Drop dough by spoonfuls into each cup.

4 Bake *15 minutes.* Invert onto tray; let pan remain over biscuits a few minutes. *1 dozen.*

SCARLETT O'HARA STRAWBERRY SHORTCAKE

Double deck extravaganza, named for fiction's beautiful Southern belle. See it on chapter cover.

1½ qt strawberries, halved
1 cup granulated sugar
4⅔ cups Bisquick baking mix
⅓ cup granulated sugar
⅓ cup butter or margarine, melted
1 cup milk
2 tbsp soft butter or margarine
½ cup brown sugar (packed)
½ cup slivered almonds
Almond Whipped Cream (right)

Heat oven to 450°

1 Stir together strawberries and 1 cup granulated sugar; set aside.

2 Stir baking mix, ⅓ cup granulated sugar, ⅓ cup butter and the milk to a soft dough. Gently smooth dough into a ball on floured cloth-covered board. Knead 8 to 10 times.

3 Divide dough in half. Pat each half into an ungreased round layer pan, 9x1½ inches. Spread each with 1 tablespoon butter; sprinkle each with ¼ cup brown sugar and ¼ cup almonds.

4 Bake *15 to 20 minutes.* Remove from pans. Place one layer top side down on serving plate; spoon half the strawberries over shortcake. Top with other layer and remaining berries. While warm, cut into serving pieces and serve with Almond Whipped Cream. *6 to 8 servings.*

ALMOND WHIPPED CREAM
In chilled bowl, beat 1 cup chilled whipping cream and 3 tablespoons sugar until stiff. Add ½ teaspoon almond extract the last minute of beating.

WINTER SHORTCAKE
Anything as good as fruit shortcake deserves to be eaten all year around. So if fresh fruit isn't available, try canned or frozen — they're good, too. For the two-layer, double-size recipe at the left, use 4 to 6 cups drained canned or thawed frozen fruit. And take your choice of apricots, blueberries, peaches, plums, raspberries, rhubarb or strawberries. Or do double berry combinations: Half strawberries and half blueberries. Or half-and-half peaches and raspberries.

SHORTCAKE BRUNCH
Here's a new ruffle for brunchtime entertaining. Make a whole meal of creamy, golden-crusted strawberry shortcake. And pass a variety of toppings—a pitcher of rich cream, a bowl of Almond Whipped Cream (left), another bowl of softened ice cream.

GUACAMOLE DIP

Hot and peppery version of the classic recipe from the colorful Southwest. For a Western party, serve it in a clay flowerpot lined with foil.

2 ripe avocados, peeled and
    pitted
1 medium onion, finely chopped
2 green chili peppers, finely
    chopped
1 tbsp lemon juice
1 tsp salt
½ tsp coarsely ground pepper
½ tsp ascorbic acid mixture
1 medium tomato, peeled and
    finely chopped

Mash avocados; add onion, peppers, lemon juice, salt, pepper and ascorbic acid mixture. Beat until creamy. Gently fold in tomato. Cover and refrigerate until serving time. *About 2 cups.*

TEXAS DIPPERS

A puffy kind of giant-size bread dipper for Guacamole Dip. Fun to make and eat.

2 cups Bisquick baking mix
½ cup cold water
Cornmeal

Heat fat or oil (2 to 3 inches) to 400° in deep fat fryer or kettle

1 Stir baking mix and water to a soft dough. Gently smooth dough into a ball on floured cloth-covered board. Knead 5 times.

2 Divide dough into 16 equal parts. Shape each part into a ball on board sprinkled with cornmeal. Roll each ball into a 5-inch circle.

3 Drop circles, 2 at a time, into hot fat.

4 Fry about 15 seconds on each side or until puffed and golden brown. Drain and serve warm. *16 puffs.*

ALBUQUERQUE PATIO BREAD

In 3 delicious flavors. Use chili seasoning when serving gazpacho, Italian for lasagne, cheese for fruit plate suppers.

2 cups Bisquick baking mix
⅔ cup milk
1 envelope chili seasoning mix
    (about 1½ oz) or Italian salad
    dressing mix (about ½ oz) or
    cheese sauce mix (about
    1½ oz)
Soft butter or margarine

Heat oven to 450°

1 Stir together baking mix, milk and seasoning mix; beat vigorously ½ minute.

2 Spread dough on greased baking sheet into an oblong, 8x6 inches. Spread with butter.

3 Bake *15 minutes.* While hot, cut into 24 strips, 3x¾ inch. *12 servings.*

CALIFORNIA COFFEE RING

Casual but unusual, that's Western style entertaining. So take this coffee ring to a friendly brunch and delight your guests. It's walnuts inside and out, plus caramel and orange flavors.

⅓ cup granulated sugar
1 tsp cinnamon
⅓ cup chopped walnuts
3 tbsp butter or margarine
¼ cup brown sugar (packed)
12 walnut halves
2 cups Bisquick baking mix
½ cup cold water
1 tbsp grated orange peel
¼ cup butter or margarine,
    melted

Heat oven to 400°

1 Mix granulated sugar, the cinnamon and chopped walnuts; set aside.

2 Melt 3 tablespoons butter in oven in 6½-cup ring mold; sprinkle with brown sugar. Arrange walnut halves over butter mixture.

3 Stir baking mix, water and orange peel to a soft dough.

4 Drop half of the dough by tablespoonfuls onto butter mixture and drizzle with 2 tablespoons of the butter. Sprinkle with half of the walnut mixture.

5 Drop remaining dough onto walnut mixture and drizzle with remaining butter. Sprinkle with remaining walnut mixture.

6 Bake *20 to 25 minutes.* Invert onto plate. Leave pan over coffee cake a few minutes. Serve warm. *6 to 8 servings.*

DUDE RANCH PUDDING

1 cup brown sugar (packed)
2 cups water
2 tbsp butter or margarine
¾ cup brown sugar (packed)
1¼ cups Bisquick baking mix
⅓ cup water or milk
1 cup raisins or cut-up dates
½ cup chopped nuts
1 tsp vanilla

Heat oven to 350°

1 Combine 1 cup sugar, 2 cups water and the butter in saucepan. Heat to boiling; boil 5 minutes. Pour into ungreased square pan, 8x8x2 inches.

2 Stir remaining ingredients to a soft dough. Drop dough by spoonfuls into mixture in pan. (Dough will spread as it bakes.)

3 Bake *40 to 45 minutes.* Serve warm and, if you like, with whipped cream. *9 servings.*

SUGAR BUNS HAWAII

1 can (8½ oz) crushed
   pineapple, drained
½ cup soft butter or margarine
½ cup brown sugar (packed)
1 tsp cinnamon, if desired
2⅓ cups Bisquick baking mix
3 tbsp granulated sugar
3 tbsp butter or margarine,
   melted
½ cup milk

Heat oven to 425°

1 Mix pineapple, ½ cup butter, the brown sugar and cinnamon. Divide evenly among 12 greased medium muffin cups.

2 Stir baking mix, granulated sugar, 3 tablespoons butter and the milk to a soft dough.

3 Spoon dough over pineapple mixture in muffin cups.

4 Bake *15 to 20 minutes.* Immediately invert onto tray. Serve warm. *1 dozen.*

TUCSON DATE COOKIES

Date Filling (below)
½ cup butter or margarine,
   softened
1¼ cups brown sugar (packed)
2 eggs
1 tsp vanilla
3½ cups Bisquick baking mix

1 Prepare Date Filling. Cool.

2 Heat oven to 375°. Mix butter and sugar; stir in eggs, vanilla and baking mix.

3 Drop dough by teaspoonfuls onto ungreased baking sheet; spread slightly. Top with Date Filling. Drop small amount of dough onto Date Filling.

4 Bake *10 to 12 minutes* or until light brown. *About 4 dozen.*

DATE FILLING Mix 1½ cups cut-up dates (8 ounces), ½ cup sugar and ½ cup water in small saucepan. Cook over medium heat, stirring constantly, until thickened. Stir in ¼ cup chopped nuts.

ALASKA SALMON SUPPER

Alaska's Indians still cook the whole split salmon outdoors, secured to a sapling and roasted over glowing coals. If you don't have time to be authentic, try this for speed.

⅓ cup chopped green pepper
3 tbsp chopped onion
3 tbsp shortening
¼ cup Bisquick baking mix
1 can (10½ oz) condensed
  cream of celery soup
¾ cup milk
1 can (7¾ oz) salmon, drained
1 cup drained cooked peas
1 tbsp lemon juice
1 cup Bisquick baking mix
¼ cup cold water

Heat oven to 450°

1 Cook and stir pepper and onion in shortening in large saucepan over medium heat until tender. Stir in ¼ cup baking mix. Gradually stir in soup and milk. Heat to boiling, stirring constantly. Boil and stir 1 minute. Stir in salmon, peas and lemon juice.

2 Pour mixture into ungreased square pan, 8x8x2 inches. Keep hot in oven while preparing biscuits.

3 Stir 1 cup baking mix and the water to a soft dough. Drop dough by 5 or 6 spoonfuls onto hot salmon mixture.

4 Bake *about 15 minutes. 5 or 6 servings.*

APPLE WASHINGTON

A speedy version of Apple Betty, renamed for Washington State—the Apple Bowl of the World. Try it with ice cream on top.

1 cup Bisquick baking mix
1 cup brown sugar (packed)
½ tsp cinnamon
¼ cup butter or margarine,
  softened
5 cups sliced pared apples
  (about 5 medium)

Heat oven to 375°

1 Mix all ingredients except apples; set aside. Place apples in ungreased square pan, 9x9x2 inches.

2 Sprinkle sugar mixture over apples.

3 Bake *30 minutes* or until apples are tender. Serve warm. *6 servings.*

RASPBERRY CHIFFON PIE

Can you improve upon anything as good as the Northwest's raspberries? Try this for sighs—ruby red raspberries folded into chiffon filling and set to chill in a short pie shell.

9-INCH SHORT PIE SHELL

1 cup Bisquick baking mix
¼ cup butter or margarine, softened
3 tbsp boiling water

Heat oven to 450°

1 Combine baking mix and butter in small bowl. Add water; stir vigorously until dough forms a ball and cleans the bowl. (Dough will be puffy and soft.)

2 Pat dough with floured hands into 9-inch pie pan, bringing up dough to edge of pan. If you like, flute edge.

3 Bake *8 to 10 minutes.* Cool.

FILLING

¼ cup sugar
1 envelope unflavored gelatin
1 pkg (10 oz) frozen raspberries, thawed
3 egg whites
¼ tsp cream of tartar
⅓ cup sugar
½ cup chilled whipping cream

Stir together ¼ cup sugar, the gelatin and raspberries (with syrup) in saucepan. Cook over medium heat, stirring constantly, just until mixture boils. Place pan in bowl of ice and water or chill in refrigerator, stirring occasionally, until mixture mounds when dropped from a spoon. Beat egg whites and cream of tartar until foamy. Beat in ⅓ cup sugar, 1 tablespoon at a time; continue beating until stiff and glossy. Do not underbeat. In chilled bowl, beat cream until stiff. Fold whipped cream and berry mixture into meringue. Pile into pie shell. Chill at least 4 hours or until set.

OREGON PEARS AU CHOCOLAT   Chill 1 can (15 ounces) pear halves. For each serving, put 2 pear halves, well drained, together with 1 tablespoon Betty Crocker canned chocolate frosting. Place pear upright in dessert dish. Top each with chocolate sauce made by melting more frosting over hot water. Garnish with maraschino cherry and you have Oregon's two famous fruits in one dessert.

MIDWEST TOMATO SHORTCAKES

Minneapolis is the home of Bisquick baking mix and speedy biscuit shortcakes. Here we combine them with bacon, tomato and Wisconsin Cheese Sauce for a superb main dish surprise.

Wisconsin Cheese Sauce (right)
2⅓ cups Bisquick baking mix
3 tbsp butter or margarine, melted
½ cup milk
Soft butter or margarine
3 medium tomatoes, thinly sliced
6 slices bacon, crisply fried

Heat oven to 450°

1 Prepare Wisconsin Cheese Sauce. Cover to keep warm.

2 Stir baking mix, 3 tablespoons butter and the milk to a soft dough. Gently smooth dough into a ball on floured cloth-covered board. Knead 8 to 10 times.

3 Roll dough ½ inch thick. Cut with floured 3-inch cutter.

4 Bake on ungreased baking sheet *about 10 minutes.*

To serve, split shortcakes horizontally; spread halves with butter. Place tomato slices between layers and on top of each shortcake. Spoon warm cheese sauce over shortcakes and garnish each with a bacon slice. *6 servings.*

DAIRYLAND SUPPER
Midwest Tomato Shortcakes
   with Wisconsin Cheese
   Sauce
Buttered Broccoli
Ice-cream Sundaes
Coffee   Milk

WISCONSIN CHEESE SAUCE

3 tbsp butter or margarine
3 tbsp Bisquick baking mix
¼ tsp salt
¼ tsp dry mustard
⅛ tsp thyme
⅛ tsp pepper
1½ cups milk
1½ cups shredded process sharp Cheddar cheese (about 6 oz)

Melt butter over low heat in saucepan. Blend in baking mix and seasonings. Cook over low heat, stirring until mixture is smooth and bubbly. Remove from heat and stir in milk. Heat to boiling, stirring constantly. Boil and stir 1 minute. Stir in cheese. Heat over low heat, stirring constantly, until cheese is melted.

HAMBURGER ONION BUNS

Think how great grilled hamburgers would taste on your own homemade onion buns? Go ahead, show off a little.

1 pkg active dry yeast
1 cup warm water (105 to 115°)
4 cups Bisquick baking mix
2 tbsp sugar
2 tbsp onion flakes
Soft butter or margarine

1 Dissolve yeast in warm water in large mixer bowl. Add 2 cups of the baking mix and the sugar. Blend ½ minute on low speed, scraping bowl constantly. Beat 2 minutes medium speed, scraping bowl frequently. (By hand, beat 300 vigorous strokes.)

2 Stir in remaining baking mix and the onion flakes until smooth. Scrape batter from side of bowl. Cover and let rise in warm place until double, about 30 minutes. Stir down batter by beating 25 strokes.

3 Drop batter by 12 spoonfuls about 2 inches apart onto greased baking sheet. Flatten mounds into rounds about ½ inch thick with floured hand. Cover and let rise in warm place 40 minutes.

4 Heat oven to 400°. Bake *12 to 15 minutes* or until nicely browned. While hot, brush tops of buns with butter. *1 dozen.*

IOWA CORN FRITTERS

How long has it been since you've had real homemade corn fritters? With maple syrup or confectioners' sugar. Why not fry up a batch tonight?

2 cups Bisquick baking mix
½ cup cold water
1 egg
1 can (17 oz) whole kernel corn, drained (2 cups)
Syrup or confectioners' sugar

Heat fat or oil (2 to 3 inches) to 375° in deep fat fryer or kettle

1 Stir together baking mix, water and egg until smooth. Stir in corn.

2 Drop batter by small spoonfuls into hot fat.

3 Fry until golden brown on both sides. Drain and serve hot with syrup. *About 2 dozen.*

PRAIRIE CRESCENTS

From the wheat fields of Dakota—a yeast bread recipe for tender, flaky rolls. Made convenient with Bisquick baking mix.

1 pkg active dry yeast
⅔ cup warm water (105 to 115°)
2 tbsp sugar
2 tbsp shortening
2½ cups Bisquick baking mix
Soft butter or margarine

1 Dissolve yeast in warm water. Stir in sugar, shortening and baking mix; beat vigorously.

2 Turn dough onto floured board. Knead until smooth, about 20 times.

3 Roll dough into 12-inch circle. Cut into 16 wedges. Roll up, beginning at rounded edge. Place rolls with points underneath on lightly greased baking sheet. Cover and let rise in warm place until double, about 30 minutes.

4 Heat oven to 400°. Bake *10 to 15 minutes* or until golden brown. While hot, brush with butter. *16 rolls.*

U.S.A. FUDGE SQUARES

These are rich, triple-decker brownie treats—favorites of chocolate lovers from coast to coast for teatime or snacktime.

2 squares (1 oz each)
    unsweetened chocolate
¼ cup butter or margarine
¾ cup sugar
2 eggs
1½ cups Bisquick baking mix
½ cup chopped nuts
Topping (right)
1½ squares unsweetened
    chocolate

Heat oven to 350°

1 Melt 2 squares chocolate and the butter in medium saucepan over low heat. Stir in sugar, eggs, baking mix and nuts.

2 Spread dough in greased square pan, 9x9x2 inches.

3 Bake *25 to 30 minutes.* Do not overbake. Cool and spread with Topping. Refrigerate.

4 Melt 1½ squares chocolate over low heat; cool slightly. Spread evenly over Topping. Refrigerate about 1 hour. Cut into 1-inch squares. Store in refrigerator. *81 squares.*

TOPPING Blend 2 cups confectioners' sugar, ¼ cup soft butter or margarine, 1 tablespoon milk and 1 teaspoon vanilla.

NOTE For after-school snacks, serve them with ice cream. Very good for your mother image.

FOREIGN FLAIR

FOREIGN FLAIR

Where in the world would you like to go via a recipe? To the British Isles for Olde English Trifle or Welsh Pasties. Tokyo for Tempura. Or, how about Gay Paree for Cherry Crêpes Flambé? Then again, maybe you'd like to cover two continents in one day — say, a trip to Sweden for a coffee break and a stopover in México for supper. The recommended bill-of-fare, in that case, Swedish Kaffekrans and Chili Enchiladas.

These are the foreign borns from our recipe collection. Some are traditional favorites, others gourmet classics. And to provide a shortcut to Foreign Flair, we've adapted these recipes to American methods with Bisquick baking mix. This is the way, we say, to go gourmet gradually — and to coddle tastes to new experiences. Another way to broaden children's horizons is to discuss these foods and the lands they come from. It stimulates conversation at mealtime as well as appetites.

Bon voyage and happy eating all the way!

Betty Crocker

Cherry Crêpes Flambé is pictured on the other side of this page. The recipe is on page 108.

BELGIAN WAFFLES

An elegant, internationally inspired dessert — made famous at the New York World's Fair in the 60's.

2 eggs
1 cup milk
2⅓ cups Bisquick baking mix
2 tbsp granulated sugar
¼ cup salad oil
1 cup chilled whipping cream
¼ cup confectioners' sugar
2 cups sliced fresh strawberries
    or 1 pkg (16 oz) frozen sliced
    strawberries, thawed and
    drained
Confectioners' sugar

1 Beat eggs in small mixer bowl on high speed 5 minutes or until thick and lemon colored. Stir in milk, baking mix, granulated sugar and oil.

2 Pour batter from cup or pitcher onto center of hot waffle iron.

3 Bake until steaming stops. Remove waffle carefully and break into sections.

4 In chilled bowl, beat cream and ¼ cup confectioners' sugar until stiff; fold in strawberries. Put waffle sections together in pairs with whipped cream mixture. Sprinkle each waffle sandwich with confectioners' sugar. *6 servings.*

BELGIAN COFFEE   Spoon creamy, sweetened meringue into heated cups. Then top with strong coffee.

IRISH SODA BREAD

The pride of Ireland made an easy modern way. A caraway and raisin adaptation. Good, quick and inexpensive.

1 cup Bisquick baking mix
¼ cup raisins
1 tsp caraway seed
⅓ cup milk

Heat oven to 450°

1 Mix all ingredients.

2 Spread dough in greased 8-inch pie pan.

3 Bake *about 12 minutes* or until golden. Cut into wedges; serve hot and, if you like, with butter. *4 to 6 servings.*

LONDON BUNS

Rich fruit muffins — like those enjoyed by generations of British schoolboys.

2 cups Bisquick baking mix
¼ cup sugar
½ cup milk
1 egg
2 tbsp butter, melted, or salad oil
1 cup currants or raisins
½ cup candied fruit

Heat oven to 400°

1 Mix all ingredients; beat vigorously ½ minute.

2 Fill 16 greased medium or 20 small muffin cups or paper-lined muffin cups ⅔ full.

3 Bake *12 to 15 minutes* or until golden brown. Serve hot.
16 medium or 20 small muffins.

OLDE ENGLISH TRIFLE

From the land of Dickens, Churchill and the Beatles comes this old-time dessert — a custardy, chilled cake with wine-fruit flavor.

1½ cups Bisquick baking mix
½ cup granulated sugar
1 egg
½ cup milk or water
2 tbsp shortening
1 tsp vanilla
½ cup raspberry jam
⅓ cup sherry or sherry flavoring
1 can (18 oz) Betty Crocker vanilla pudding
⅓ cup toasted slivered almonds
¾ cup chilled whipping cream
3 tbsp confectioners' sugar

Heat oven to 350°

1 Blend baking mix, granulated sugar, egg, milk, shortening and vanilla in large mixer bowl on low speed ½ minute, scraping bowl frequently. Beat 4 minutes medium speed.

2 Pour batter into greased and floured square pan, 8x8x2 inches.

3 Bake *30 to 35 minutes* or until wooden pick inserted in center comes out clean. Cool.

4 Cut cake into 9 or 12 pieces. Split pieces and fill with jam. Place in baking dish, 11½x7½x1½ inches. Sprinkle with wine. Pour pudding over cake and sprinkle with almonds.

5 In chilled bowl, beat cream and confectioners' sugar until stiff; spread on cake. Chill at least 4 hours. If you like, garnish with chopped candied cherries. Cut into servings.
9 to 12 servings.

SCOTCH SCONES

Tea and scones — a Highland favorite. Sweet, rich biscuit dough that you shape and bake into toasty triangles.

2 cups Bisquick baking mix
¼ cup sugar
2 eggs
2 tbsp butter or margarine, melted

Heat oven to 400°

1 Stir baking mix, sugar and eggs to a soft dough. Gently smooth dough into a ball on floured cloth-covered board. Knead 5 times.

2 Roll dough ¼ inch thick. Cut into 2-inch squares; brush with butter. Fold each square into a triangle; lightly seal edges. Place on ungreased baking sheet. If you like, brush triangles with slightly beaten egg white.

3 Bake *6 to 8 minutes* or until golden brown. *About 1½ dozen.*

WELSH PASTIES

For appetizers or a simple supper. Serve with chili sauce.

1 cup chopped cooked corned beef
¼ cup chopped onion
¼ cup shredded Cheddar cheese
3 to 6 drops red pepper sauce
1 cup Bisquick baking mix
¼ cup cold water

Heat oven to 450°

1 Mix beef, onion, cheese and pepper sauce; set aside.

2 Stir baking mix and water to a soft dough. Gently smooth dough into a ball on floured cloth-covered board. Knead 5 times.

3 Roll dough into a rectangle, 12x6 inches. Cut into eight 3-inch squares.

4 Spoon meat mixture on center of each square. Fold dough over to make triangles and press edges together to seal.

5 Bake on ungreased baking sheet *about 10 minutes. 8 pasties.*

CHERRY CRÊPES FLAMBÉ

The French have a way with flaming crêpes — and so can you! This recipe takes you step by step to a dramatic finish for a posh party. See it pictured on the chapter cover.

1 cup dairy sour cream
⅓ cup brown sugar (packed)
1 cup Bisquick baking mix
1 egg
1 cup milk
1 can (21 oz) cherry pie filling
¼ cup orange-flavored liqueur

Heat oven to 350°

1 Blend sour cream and brown sugar; set aside.

2 Beat baking mix, egg and milk with rotary beater until smooth.

3 Spoon 2 tablespoons batter into hot lightly greased 6- or 7-inch skillet. Rotate pan until batter covers bottom.

4 Bake until bubbles appear. Gently loosen edge; turn and bake other side.

5 Spoon 1 tablespoon sour cream mixture onto one half of each crêpe; roll up. Place crêpes seam side down on ovenproof platter.

6 Bake *about 5 minutes.* Heat pie filling in chafing dish until warm. Heat liqueur in small saucepan until warm. Slowly pour liqueur over pie filling. Do not stir. Ignite immediately and spoon over crêpes. *12 to 15 crêpes.*

DRAMA WITH A CHAFING DISH For a successful flaming dessert, don't boil or overheat the liqueur — and don't stir the warmed liqueur into the cherries. Do as the recipe says, then dim the lights and perform.

CREAM PUFFS

French pastry made easy.

¾ cup water
¼ cup butter or margarine
1 cup Bisquick baking mix
4 eggs

Heat oven to 400°

1 Heat water and butter to a rolling boil in large saucepan. Add baking mix all at once. Stir vigorously over low heat about 1½ minutes or until mixture forms a ball. Remove from heat and beat in eggs, one at a time; continue beating until smooth.

2 Drop dough by rounded tablespoonfuls 2 inches apart onto aluminum foil-covered baking sheet.

3 Bake *25 to 30 minutes.* Cool. Fill with Betty Crocker vanilla pudding or sweetened whipped cream and refrigerate. *About 2 dozen.*

CRÊPES WITH CRABMEAT

Another pancake classic. This time crêpes become a main dish served with crabmeat and the famous Mornay Sauce. Add a salad and you have a party menu.

Mornay Sauce (right)
1 can (7½ oz) crabmeat, drained
    and cartilage removed
½ tsp salt
⅛ tsp garlic salt
¼ tsp grated lemon peel
1 cup Bisquick baking mix
1 egg
1 cup milk
Paprika
Slivered almonds

Heat oven to 350°

1 Prepare Mornay Sauce. Cover to keep warm.

2 Mix crabmeat, salt, garlic salt, lemon peel and ¼ cup Mornay Sauce; set aside.

3 Beat baking mix, egg and milk with rotary beater until smooth.

4 Spoon 2 tablespoons batter into hot lightly greased 6- or 7-inch skillet. Rotate pan until batter covers bottom.

5 Bake until bubbles appear. Gently loosen edge; turn and bake other side.

6 Spoon 1 tablespoon crabmeat mixture on center of each crêpe; roll up. Place crêpes seam side down in buttered baking dish, 11½x7½x1½ inches.

7 Bake *15 minutes.* Pour remaining Mornay Sauce over crêpes. Sprinkle with paprika and almonds.

8 Set oven control at broil and/or 550°. Broil 4 inches from heat 2 to 3 minutes or until light brown. If you like, sprinkle with parsley.
4 servings.

MORNAY SAUCE

¼ cup butter or margarine
¼ cup Bisquick baking mix
½ tsp salt
¼ tsp pepper
2 cups milk
2 cups shredded process
    American cheese (about 8 oz)

Melt butter over low heat in saucepan. Blend in baking mix and seasonings. Cook over low heat, stirring until mixture is smooth and bubbly. Remove from heat and stir in milk. Heat to boiling, stirring constantly. Boil and stir 1 minute. Stir in cheese. Heat over low heat, stirring constantly, until cheese is melted.

QUICHE LORRAINE

*A continental favorite,
supposedly invented in
Alsace-Lorraine. Serve as
first course or main dish.*

1 cup Bisquick baking mix
¼ cup light cream
12 slices bacon (½ lb), crisply
   fried and crumbled
1 cup shredded natural Swiss
   cheese (about 4 oz)
⅓ cup minced onion
4 eggs
2 cups whipping cream or
   light cream
¾ tsp salt
¼ tsp sugar
⅛ tsp cayenne pepper

Heat oven to 425°

1 Stir baking mix and light
   cream to a soft dough. Gently
   smooth dough into a ball on
   floured cloth-covered **board**.
   Knead 5 times.

2 Roll dough 2 inches larger
   than inverted 9-inch pie pan.
   Ease into pan and flute edge.

3 Sprinkle bacon, cheese and
   onion in crust. Beat remaining
   ingredients with rotary beater;
   pour over bacon mixture. Cover
   edge with 2-to 3-inch strip of
   aluminum foil to prevent
   excessive browning; remove
   foil last 15 minutes of baking.

4 Bake *15 minutes. Reduce oven
   temperature to 300°. Bake
   about 35 minutes longer* or
   until knife inserted 1 inch from
   edge comes out clean. Let
   stand 10 minutes before
   cutting. *6 servings.*

CONTINENTAL BRUNCH
Quiche Lorraine
Melon Wedges with Grapes
Petits Puffs
Café au Lait

PETITS PUFFS

*Tiny muffins, rolled in cinnamon
and sugar.*

⅔ cup sugar
1 tsp cinnamon
2 cups Bisquick baking mix
¼ cup sugar
¼ tsp nutmeg
2 tbsp butter or margarine,
   softened
1 egg
½ cup milk
½ cup butter or margarine,
   melted

Heat oven to 400°

1 Mix ⅔ cup sugar and the
   cinnamon; set aside.

2 Combine baking mix, ¼ cup
   sugar, the nutmeg, 2
   tablespoons butter, the egg
   and milk; beat vigorously
   ½ minute.

3 Fill 24 greased tiny muffin cups
   ⅔ full.

4 Bake *10 minutes.* Immediately
   roll in ½ cup melted butter,
   then in sugar mixture. Serve
   warm. *2 dozen.*

FRUIT KUCHEN

Borrowed from Germany — coffee cake with a rich, fruity topping.

2 cups Bisquick baking mix
2 tbsp sugar
1 egg
⅔ cup water or milk
1 cup well-drained cut-up fruit
Streusel Topping (below)

Heat oven to 400°

1 Combine baking mix, sugar, egg and water; beat vigorously ½ minute.

2 Spread batter in greased square pan, 9x9x2 inches. Spoon fruit evenly over batter; sprinkle with Streusel Topping.

3 Bake *20 to 25 minutes.* Serve warm. *9 to 12 servings.*

STREUSEL TOPPING Mix ⅓ cup Bisquick baking mix, ⅓ cup brown sugar (packed), ½ teaspoon cinnamon and 2 tablespoons firm butter or margarine until crumbly.

PARMESAN-WINE SUPPER BREAD

Bread, fruit and wine make a meal. Especially when the flavors of Italy are baked in the bread.

1½ cups Bisquick baking mix
1 tbsp sugar
1 tbsp instant minced onion
1 egg
¼ cup milk
¼ cup white wine or apple juice
½ tsp oregano
¼ cup grated Parmesan cheese

Heat oven to 400°

1 Mix all ingredients except cheese to a soft dough.

2 Spread dough in greased round layer pan, 8x1½ inches. Sprinkle with cheese.

3 Bake *20 to 25 minutes.* Cut into wedges; serve warm. *6 to 8 servings.*

CHILI ENCHILADAS

The food of old México. Make the tortillas ahead. Turn them into enchiladas with a filling of chili, onion and cheese.

TORTILLAS
1 cup Bisquick baking mix
¼ cup cold water
Cornmeal

1 Stir baking mix and water to a soft dough. Gently smooth dough into a ball on floured cloth-covered board. Knead 5 times.

2 Divide dough into 8 equal parts. Shape each part into a ball. Roll each into a 5-inch circle on board dusted with cornmeal.

3 Bake on hot ungreased griddle about 1 minute on each side. *8 tortillas.*

NOTE To keep tortillas from drying, place them between the folds of a damp towel.

FILLING
2 cans (15½ oz each) chili
without beans
¼ cup chopped onion
2 cups shredded process
American cheese (about 8 oz)

Heat oven to 350°

Mix 1 can chili, 2 tablespoons of the onion and 1 cup of the cheese. Spoon about ⅓ cup of the chili mixture on center of each tortilla. Roll up; place seam side down in ungreased baking dish, 11½ x 7½ x 1½ inches. Spoon remaining chili over tortillas; sprinkle with remaining onion and cheese. Bake *20 minutes* or until cheese is melted. *4 to 6 servings.*

TORTILLAS ALONE A novelty for the party bread plate. Serve hot, spread with butter and roll them up to eat.

LAS TOSTADAS

Tortillas, taco sauce and cheese combine for cocktail appetizers.

Tortillas (page 112)
1 can (4 oz) sauce for tacos
1 cup shredded Cheddar cheese
   (about 4 oz)

Set oven control at broil and/or 550°. Spread each tortilla with sauce; sprinkle with cheese. Broil 5 inches from heat about 1 minute or until bubbly. Serve warm as appetizers.

SANGRÍA   In glass pitcher, combine ⅔ cup lemon juice and ⅓ cup orange juice, strained. Add ¼ cup sugar, stirring until dissolved. Just before serving, pour in 1 bottle (4/5 quart) red wine and stir again. Add ice and large twists of lemon and orange peel. Serve in punch cups. *6 to 8 servings (about ½ cup each).*

MEXICAN FIESTA CASSEROLE

Familiar flavors of México — green peppers, tomatoes and ground beef — combined with a rich sour cream mixture and biscuit dough. Delicioso.

1 lb ground beef
1 cup dairy sour cream
⅔ cup mayonnaise or salad
   dressing
1 cup shredded sharp Cheddar
   cheese (about 4 oz)
2 tbsp chopped onion
2 cups Bisquick baking mix
½ cup cold water
2 to 3 medium tomatoes, thinly
   sliced
¾ cup chopped green pepper

Heat oven to 375°

1 Cook and stir ground beef until brown; drain and set aside. Mix sour cream, mayonnaise, cheese and onion; set aside.

2 Stir baking mix and water to a soft dough.

3 Pat dough in greased oblong pan, 13x9x2 inches, pressing dough ½ inch up sides of pan.

4 Layer ground beef, tomatoes and green pepper; spoon sour cream mixture over top. If you like, sprinkle with paprika.

5 Bake *25 to 30 minutes* or until edges of dough are light brown. *10 servings.*

MEXICAN SUPPER
Chili Enchiladas or Mexican
   Fiesta Casserole
Shredded Lettuce and
   Chopped Tomatoes
Fresh Fruit
Cold Beer

CHINESE ALMOND COOKIES

Modern version of the old Chinese cookie. Nice with tea after Tempura.

1¾ cups Bisquick baking mix
½ cup sugar
¼ cup shortening
1 egg
½ tsp almond extract
About 30 unblanched almonds

Heat oven to 350°

1 Mix all ingredients except almonds to a stiff dough. Work with hands until dough holds together.

2 Shape dough by table-spoonfuls into 1-inch balls. Place 2 inches apart on greased baking sheet. Flatten each to ¼ inch with lightly floured bottom of glass. Press almond into center of each.

3 Bake *12 to 15 minutes* or until light brown. *About 2½ dozen.*

TEMPURA

An easy way to go gourmet.

1½ cups Bisquick baking mix
1 egg
¾ cup cold water
Dippers (below)
Sauce (below)
Grated radish, drained

Heat fat or oil (2 inches) to 350° in electric skillet

1 Stir baking mix, egg and water until smooth.

2 Dip choice of Dippers into batter, allowing excess batter to drip into bowl.

3 Fry in hot fat about 1 minute on each side or until golden brown. Drain. Dip foods into Sauce and then into radish. *6 servings.*

DIPPERS Cooked shrimp, lean pork cubes. Green pepper, celery and carrot strips. Sliced fresh mushrooms Pineapple chunks.

SAUCE Blend ½ cup soy sauce, ½ cup lemon juice and ¼ cup sherry.

SOUTH SEA MUFFINS

*With the tropical flavors of
pineapple and sugar cane
country.*

2 cups Bisquick baking mix
¼ cup sugar
2 tbsp butter or margarine,
    softened
1 egg
⅔ cup milk
½ cup well-drained crushed
    pineapple
Thin Icing (below)
Chopped nuts

Heat oven to 400°

1 Combine baking mix, sugar,
butter, egg and milk; beat
vigorously ½ minute. Fold in
pineapple.

2 Fill 48 greased tiny muffin
cups ⅔ full.

3 Bake *12 to 15 minutes.* While
warm, frost with Thin Icing and
sprinkle with nuts. *4 dozen.*

THIN ICING   Blend ½ cup
confectioners' sugar and
1 tablespoon water.

TAHITIAN CAKE

*A simple one-layer cake with
two luscious toppings. First,
coconut and macadamia nuts;
then Banana Whip.*

1½ cups Bisquick baking mix
½ cup sugar
1 egg
½ cup milk or water
2 tbsp shortening
1 tsp vanilla
Coconut-Macadamia Topping
    (right)
Banana Whip (right)
Whole strawberries

Heat oven to 350°

1 Blend baking mix, sugar, egg,
milk, shortening and vanilla in
large mixer bowl on low speed
½ minute, scraping bowl
frequently. Beat 4 minutes
medium speed.

2 Pour batter into greased and
floured square pan, 8x8x2
inches.

3 Bake *30 to 35 minutes* or until
wooden pick inserted in
center comes out clean. While
warm, spread with Coconut-
Macadamia Topping.

4 Set oven control at broil
and/or 550°. Place cake about
3 inches from heat; broil
about 3 minutes or until
mixture is nicely browned.
Cool. Top each serving with
Banana Whip and a strawberry.

COCONUT-MACADAMIA
TOPPING   Mix 3 tablespoons
soft butter or margarine, ⅓
cup brown sugar (packed), 2
tablespoons light cream, ½
cup flaked coconut and ¼ cup
chopped macadamia nuts.

BANANA WHIP   Prepare 1
envelope (about 2 ounces)
dessert topping mix as
directed on package except —
fold in 1 ripe banana, mashed.

BEEF STROGANOFF CASSEROLE

A Russian import turned into a casserole — with vegetables and sour cream biscuits added. It takes a little time, but think what it can do for your hostess reputation.

½ cup Bisquick baking mix
½ tsp salt
⅛ tsp pepper
⅛ tsp paprika
1½ lb beef stew meat,
    cut into 1-inch cubes
2 tbsp shortening
½ cup chopped onion
1 cup sliced carrots
1 clove garlic, minced
1 can (16 oz) tomatoes
⅔ cup dairy sour cream
1 tsp salt
⅛ tsp pepper
2 cups Bisquick baking mix
⅓ cup dairy sour cream
1 tbsp snipped chives
⅓ cup cold water

1 Blend ½ cup baking mix, ½ teaspoon salt, ⅛ teaspoon pepper and the paprika; coat meat.

2 Cook meat in shortening in large skillet until brown. Stir in onion, carrots, garlic, tomatoes, ⅔ cup sour cream, 1 teaspoon salt and ⅛ teaspoon pepper; cover tightly.

3 Cook over low heat 1½ to 2 hours or until meat is tender.

4 Heat oven to 425°. Turn meat mixture into ungreased 2-quart casserole. Keep hot in oven while preparing biscuits.

5 Stir 2 cups baking mix, ⅓ cup sour cream, the chives and water to a soft dough. Gently smooth dough into a ball on floured cloth-covered board. Knead 5 times.

6 Roll dough ½ inch thick. Cut with floured 2-inch cutter. Place biscuits on hot meat mixture.

7 Bake *15 to 20 minutes* or until biscuits are golden brown. *6 servings.*

KOLACHES

A sweet bun filled with jam or jelly. Inspired by the Czechs, simplified by Bisquick baking mix.

2⅓ cups Bisquick baking mix
3 tbsp sugar
3 tbsp butter or margarine,
    melted
½ cup milk
About ½ cup jam or jelly

Heat oven to 425°

1 Stir baking mix, sugar, butter and milk to a soft dough. Gently smooth dough into a ball on floured cloth-covered board. Knead 8 to 10 times.

2 Roll dough ½ inch thick. Cut with floured 3-inch cutter; place on ungreased baking sheet. With floured fingers, press a deep indentation about 2 inches in diameter in center of each. Fill with about 1 tablespoon jam.

3 Bake *about 10 minutes* or until light brown. *6 kolaches.*

SWEDISH KAFFEKRANS

Like the popular yeast bread coffee cakes of Sweden, only faster. So pretty it can double as centerpiece at brunch.

⅓ cup brown sugar (packed)
  or granulated sugar
⅓ cup raisins
2 tsp cinnamon
1 pkg active dry yeast
½ cup warm water (105 to 115°)
1 egg
1 tbsp granulated sugar
2½ cups Bisquick baking mix
2 tbsp soft butter or margarine
Confectioners' Icing (right)

1   Mix ⅓ cup sugar, the raisins and cinnamon; set aside.

2   Dissolve yeast in warm water. Mix in egg, 1 tablespoon granulated sugar and the baking mix; beat vigorously.

3   Turn dough onto floured board. Knead until smooth, about 20 times.

4   Roll dough into a rectangle, 16x9 inches. Spread rectangle with butter; sprinkle with raisin mixture. Roll up tightly, beginning at wide side. Seal well by pinching edge of dough into roll.

5   Place dough seam side down in a circle on greased baking sheet; pinch ends together. Make cuts ⅔ of the way through ring at 1-inch intervals; turn each section on its side. Cover and let rise in warm place until double, about 1 hour.

6   Heat oven to 375°. Bake *15 minutes* or until light brown. While warm, frost with Confectioners' Icing. Serve warm.

CONFECTIONERS' ICING
Blend 1 cup confectioners' sugar, 1 to 2 teaspoons water and ½ teaspoon vanilla.

DANISH AEBLESKIVER

If you have the cast-iron aebleskiver pan, try these novel little pancake balls served with applesauce.

5 eggs, separated
2 cups Bisquick baking mix
¾ cup milk
Butter or margarine
Confectioners' sugar
Applesauce

1 Beat egg whites in large mixer bowl on high speed until stiff but not dry; set aside.

2 Blend egg yolks, baking mix and milk in small mixer bowl on low speed. Fold egg yolk mixture into beaten egg whites.

3 Butter each cup in aebleskiver pan. Heat pan over medium heat. Fill cups ⅔ full.

4 Bake until bubbly; turn carefully with metal skewer or small spatula and bake other side until golden brown. While warm, sprinkle with sugar and serve with applesauce. *About 40.*

SWEDISH DESSERT PANCAKES

Scandinavian plättar, like French crêpes, are tender, light and rich.

1¼ cups Bisquick baking mix
3 eggs
1¾ cups milk
¼ cup butter or margarine, melted
Jam, sugar, applesauce or whipped cream

1 Beat all ingredients except jam with rotary beater until smooth.

2 Spoon about 3 tablespoons batter into hot lightly greased 6- or 7-inch skillet. Rotate pan until batter covers bottom.

3 Bake until bubbles appear. Gently loosen edge; turn and bake other side.

4 Spread each pancake with jam; roll up. If you like, sprinkle with confectioners' sugar. Serve warm. *About 15.*

SWISS CHEESE STARS

Cheese-flavored biscuit appetizers, cut into star shapes with a cookie cutter. Serve with wine or mugs of cider.

1 cup Bisquick baking mix
⅓ cup milk
1 cup shredded Swiss cheese (about 4 oz)
Paprika

Heat oven to 450°

1 Stir baking mix, milk and cheese to a soft dough. Gently smooth dough into a ball on floured cloth-covered board. Knead 5 times.

2 Roll dough ¼ inch thick; cut into star shapes with cookie cutter. Sprinkle with paprika.

3 Bake on ungreased baking sheet *8 to 10 minutes.* Serve warm. *1½ dozen.*

BISCUITS*

2 cups Bisquick baking mix
½ cup cold water

Heat oven to 450°

1 Stir ingredients to a soft dough. Gently smooth dough into a ball on floured cloth-covered board. Knead 5 times.

2 Roll dough ½ inch thick. Cut with floured 2-inch cutter.

3 Bake on ungreased baking sheet *8 to 10 minutes. 10 to 12 biscuits.*

DROP BISCUITS Do not knead dough; drop by spoonfuls onto greased baking sheet. *10 biscuits.*

*For altitudes over 4,000 feet, follow directions except — increase oven temperature 25°.

COFFEE CAKE*

2 cups Bisquick baking mix
2 tbsp sugar
1 egg
⅔ cup water or milk
Streusel Topping (below)

Heat oven to 400°

1 Combine all ingredients except topping; beat vigorously ½ minute.

2 Spread batter in greased round layer pan, 9x1½ inches. Sprinkle with Streusel Topping.

3 Bake *20 to 25 minutes.* Serve warm. *8 servings.*

STREUSEL TOPPING Mix ⅓ cup Bisquick baking mix, ⅓ cup brown sugar (packed), 2 tablespoons firm butter or margarine and ½ teaspoon cinnamon until crumbly.

REGULAR SHORTCAKES*

2⅓ cups Bisquick baking mix
3 tbsp sugar
3 tbsp butter or margarine, melted
½ cup milk

Heat oven to 450°

1 Stir all ingredients to a soft dough. Gently smooth dough into a ball on floured cloth-covered board. Knead 8 to 10 times.

2 Roll dough ½ inch thick. Cut with floured 3-inch cutter.

3 Bake on ungreased baking sheet *about 10 minutes.* Split warm shortcakes. If you like, spoon fruit between and over layers; top with light cream or sweetened whipped cream. *6 servings.*

PAN SHORTCAKE Pat dough into ungreased round layer pan, 8x1½ inches. Bake *15 to 20 minutes.*

DUMPLINGS

2 cups Bisquick baking mix
⅔ cup milk

1 Stir ingredients to a soft dough.

2 Drop dough by spoonfuls onto boiling stew.

3 Cook uncovered over low heat 10 minutes; cover and cook 10 minutes longer. *10 to 12 dumplings.*

WAFFLES

2 cups Bisquick baking mix
2 tbsp salad oil
1 egg
1⅓ cups milk

1 Beat all ingredients with rotary beater until smooth.

2 Pour batter from cup or pitcher onto center of hot waffle iron.

3 Bake until steaming stops. Remove waffle carefully. *Three 9-inch waffles.*

PANCAKES

2 cups Bisquick baking mix
1 egg
1⅓ cups milk

1 Beat all ingredients with rotary beater until smooth.

2 Pour batter from ¼-cup measuring cup onto hot griddle. (Grease griddle if necessary.)

3 Bake until bubbles appear. Turn and bake other side until golden brown. *About 18.*

For thinner pancakes, stir in additional milk; for thicker pancakes, stir in additional Bisquick baking mix.

VELVET CRUMB CAKE*

1½ cups Bisquick baking mix
½ cup sugar
1 egg
½ cup milk or water
2 tbsp shortening
1 tsp vanilla

Heat oven to 350°

1 Blend all ingredients in large mixer bowl on low speed ½ minute, scraping bowl frequently. Beat 4 minutes medium speed.

2 Pour batter into greased and floured square pan, 8x8x2 inches, or round layer pan, 9x1½ inches.

3 Bake *30 to 35 minutes* or until wooden pick inserted in center comes out clean.

For broiled toppings, see page 73.

*For altitudes over 4,000 feet, follow directions except — add 2 tablespoons flour, increase liquid to ⅔ cup and bake at 375°.